God's Goodness for the Chosen

The
CHOSEN
An Interactive Bible Study
Season **4**

God's Goodness for the **Chosen**

Amanda Jenkins, Dallas Jenkins, & Douglas S. Huffman

DAVID **C** COOK

transforming lives together

GOD'S GOODNESS FOR THE CHOSEN
Published by David C Cook
4050 Lee Vance Drive
Colorado Springs, CO 80918 U.S.A.

Integrity Music Limited, a Division of David C Cook
Brighton, East Sussex BN1 2RE, England

ISBN 978-0-8307-8458-5
eISBN 978-0-8307-8459-2

The Team: Michael Covington, Stephanie Bennett, Jack Campbell, Susan Murdock, Brian Mellema, Justin Claypool
Cover Design: James Hershberger

Printed in the United States of America
First Edition 2024

1 2 3 4 5 6 7 8 9 10

122223

CONTENTS

Introduction   7

Lesson 1: Death is eclipsed by LIFE   15

Lesson 2: Grief is eclipsed by PRAISE   29

Lesson 3: Questions are eclipsed by RESOLVE   43

Lesson 4: Confusion is eclipsed by GRACE   57

Lesson 5: Temporal things are eclipsed by ETERNAL THINGS   69

Lesson 6: Heartbreak is eclipsed by LOVE   83

Lesson 7: Contamination is eclipsed by DEDICATION   97

Lesson 8: Resistance is eclipsed by RECEIVING   115

Conclusion   135

About the Authors   141

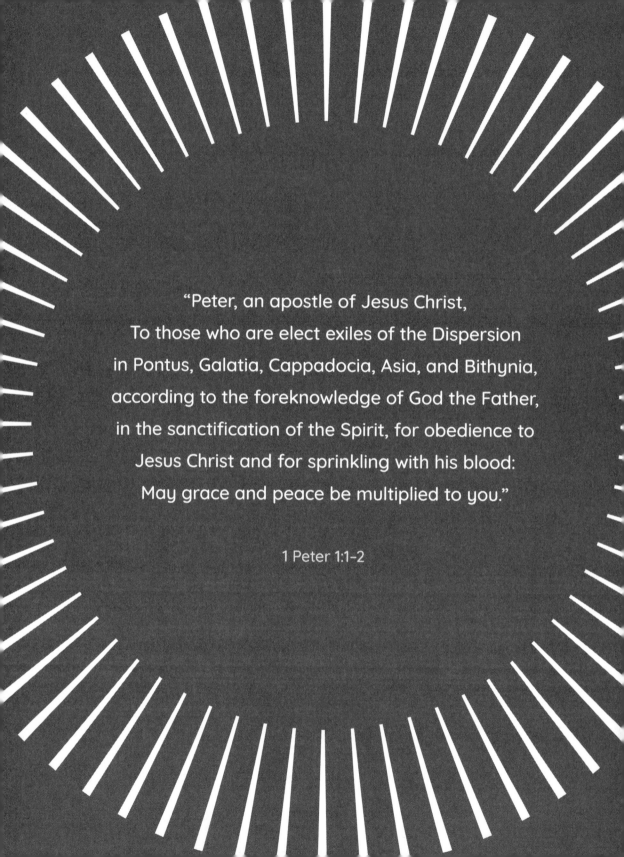

"Peter, an apostle of Jesus Christ,
To those who are elect exiles of the Dispersion
in Pontus, Galatia, Cappadocia, Asia, and Bithynia,
according to the foreknowledge of God the Father,
in the sanctification of the Spirit, for obedience to
Jesus Christ and for sprinkling with his blood:
May grace and peace be multiplied to you."

1 Peter 1:1-2

INTRODUCTION

Such an interesting way to start a letter: "To those who are elect exiles ..."

Writing in the early 60s AD, Simon Peter addressed his message to Christians who were living in parts of the first-century Middle East. He called his readers "elect exiles of the Dispersion," which means "chosen ones scattered about."

> Dispersion: the action or process of distributing things or people over a wide area.

Sound familiar? It should. Because those of us who follow Jesus *are* exiles, chosen by God and scattered about—though perhaps we don't always think of ourselves that way. Most of us haven't been overtly persecuted for following Jesus, pushed out of our homes, or threatened with death for not renouncing our faith. Peter, on the other hand, experienced all those things and, a few short years after penning this letter, was executed by the Roman emperor Nero.

The area to which Peter's letters were written

Black Sea

PONTUS

BITHYNIA

GALATIA

Aegean Sea

ASIA

CAPPADOCIA

Mediterranean Sea

Exiles:
those forced out of
their home country,
thereby having to live
somewhere else.

The Bible refers to
Christians as exiles in
the world because they
no longer belong to the
world; they belong to
the kingdom of God and
are therefore "citizens
of heaven" (Phil. 3:20).

"[Jesus] prayed, 'I am
coming to you now, but
I say these things while
I am still in the world, so
that [my followers] may
have the full measure of
my joy within them. I have
given them your word
and the world has hated
them, for they are not
of the world any more
than I am of the world.
My prayer is not that
you take them out of
the world but that you
protect them from the evil
one. They are not of the
world, even as I am not
of it. Sanctify them by the
truth; your word is truth.
As you sent me into
the world, I have sent
them into the world. For
them I sanctify myself,
that they too may be
truly sanctified.'"
John 17:13–19
(NIV)

But let's not get ahead of ourselves, because before he died, Peter lived in a way we should try to emulate. He wasn't perfect, as *The Chosen* often depicts, but he was firmly established in his faith—and it started with fish. Or, more accurately, an enormous lack thereof.

"When [Jesus] had finished speaking, he said to Simon, 'Put out into the deep and let down your nets for a catch.' And Simon answered, 'Master, we toiled all night and took nothing! But at your word I will let down the nets.' And when they had done this, they enclosed a large number of fish, and their nets were breaking. They signaled to their partners in the other boat to come and help them. And they came and filled both the boats, so that they began to sink. But when Simon Peter saw it, he fell down at Jesus' knees, saying, 'Depart from me, for I am a sinful man!' ... And Jesus said to Simon, 'Do not be afraid; from now on you will be catching men.' And when they had brought their boats to land, they left everything and followed him."

Luke 5:4–11

Consider this: Before Jesus filled Peter's boat with fish, *there were no fish*. Meaning, a professional fisherman was out all night on a fish-filled sea and caught nothing. NOTHING. And then Jesus filled his boat with so many fish, Peter couldn't haul them all in without help. Which means the miracle of the fish, as it's come to be known, was made possible because of the miracle of *the lack* of fish. The lack was a momentary suffering that was ultimately eclipsed by the bigger thing God was doing.

As a result, Peter surrendered to Jesus as Lord. Boom. Done. Except nothing is ever truly that simple, is it? Because things got a lot harder for Peter after he gave his life to Jesus. Following required him to leave his home and wife for long periods of time. It required him to minister to and serve needy people every day, no matter how he felt. It required him to live with little to no money. Or plans. Or control. Or even a complete understanding of some of the things Jesus was saying and doing.

Add to that the fierce cultural resistance of his day, jealous and dangerous religious leaders, false accusations, persistent persecution, and the ongoing oppression from Rome ... and you end up with Christ crucified and ten out of the twelve apostles turned into martyrs. Interestingly, one of Peter's last interactions with Jesus was almost identical to his first.

Only this time, it included a warning.

> "Just as day was breaking, Jesus stood on the
> shore; yet the disciples did not know that it
> was Jesus. Jesus said to them, 'Children, do you
> have any fish?' They answered him, 'No.' He
> said to them, 'Cast the net on the right side
> of the boat, and you will find some.' So they
> cast it, and now they were not able to haul it
> in, because of the quantity of fish. [John] said
> to Peter, 'It is the Lord!' When Simon Peter
> heard that it was the Lord, he ... threw himself

For Bible Nerds (like us) Who Want to Know

We know that Simon Peter lived in Capernaum (Mark 1:21–29), where he was a fisherman with his brother Andrew (Matt. 4:18; Mark 1:16), and that he was married (Matt. 8:14; Mark 1:30; Luke 4:38).

Simon is described in the New Testament as being an overly confident man who seemed to think he could earn his worth and who sometimes spoke with little forethought (Matt. 16:21–23; 26:31–35, 69–75). Luke's gospel actually makes note of such a moment, remarking after a statement made by Simon, "not knowing what he said" (Luke 9:33).

Regardless, Jesus still called him to follow (Luke 5:1–11) and was patient with him (22:31–32). Simon Peter became a key leader among the twelve apostles (Acts 1–12), bedrock preacher of the early church (Matt. 16:18), writer of two New Testament books of the Bible (1 and 2 Pet.), healer of the sick and lame (Acts 5:15), and fearless unto death (John 21:15–19).

into the sea. The other disciples came in the boat, dragging the net full of fish, for they were not far from the land, but about a hundred yards off.

When they got out on land, they saw a charcoal fire in place, with fish laid out on it, and bread. Jesus said to them, 'Bring some of the fish that you have just caught.' So Simon Peter went aboard and hauled the net ashore, full of large fish, 153 of them. And although there were so many, the net was not torn. Jesus said to them, 'Come and have breakfast.' …

When they had finished breakfast, Jesus said to Simon Peter, 'Simon, son of John, do you love me more than these?' He said to him, 'Yes, Lord; you know that I love you.' He said to him, 'Feed my lambs.' He said to him a second time, 'Simon, son of John, do you love me?' He said to him, 'Yes, Lord; you know that I love you.' He said to him, 'Tend my sheep.' He said to him the third time, 'Simon, son of John, do you love me?' Peter was grieved because he said to him the third time, 'Do you love me?' and he said to him, 'Lord, you know everything; you know that I love you.' Jesus said to him, 'Feed my sheep.

Truly, truly, I say to you, when you were young, you used to dress yourself and walk wherever you wanted, but when you are old, you will stretch out your hands, and another will dress you and carry you where you do not want to go.' (This he said to show by what kind of death he was to glorify God.) And after saying this he said to him, 'Follow me.'"

John 21:4–19

Not the world's best marketing pitch, because instead of telling His beloved disciple that following would lead to personal happiness and easier living, Jesus told Peter he would suffer. He doubled down on the hard things. *If you love Me, you'll serve. If you love Me, you'll go where I lead you. If you love Me, you'll lay down your life like I laid down Mine.* To which Peter promptly pointed at John and said, "'Lord, what about this man?' Jesus said to him, 'If it is my will that he remain until I come, what is that to you? You follow me!'" (vv. 21–22).

That's the thing about suffering—none of us want it. Peter didn't want it either, which begs the question, how did he go from being the guy who denied even knowing Jesus (Matt. 26:69–75; Luke 22:54–62) to being the guy who boldly preached the gospel no matter the consequences? How was he able to fix his eyes on the hope of heaven in spite of terrible earthly circumstances? How did he become the pillar of strength and faith he was at the end of his life?

Because time and again, Peter saw the goodness of the Lord eclipse suffering.

For Bible Nerds (like us) Who Want to Know

Who (or what) was Jesus referring to when He asked Peter, "Do you love me more than these?"

Three options have been suggested by theologians:

Option #1: "...these [things]?"

Some have argued that Jesus was referring to nearby fishing paraphernalia (boats, nets, gear) since Peter had just said, "I am going fishing" (John 21:3).

But the choice between material things and the risen Savior seems ridiculous. So, that probably wasn't what Jesus meant.

Option #2: "...these [people]?"

Some have argued that Jesus meant, "Do you love me more than you love these other disciples?"

But the choice between loving other people and loving the risen Lord Jesus (who the other disciples loved too) also seems ridiculous. So, that probably wasn't what Jesus meant.

Option #3: "...these [people do]?" We believe Jesus was asking, "Do you love me more than these other disciples love me?"

Of course, it wasn't a competition over who loved Jesus more. But Peter had boasted, "I will lay down my life for you," right before Jesus predicted that he would actually deny Jesus three times:

Simon Peter asked him, "Lord, where are you going?" Jesus replied, "Where I am going, you cannot follow now, but you will follow later." Peter asked, "Lord, why can't I follow you now? I will lay down my life for you." Then Jesus answered, "Will you really lay down your life for me? Very truly I tell you, before the rooster crows, you will disown me three times!" (John 13:36–38 NIV).

In that context, we could probably expand Jesus's question to, "Now that you have denied me three times, just like I said you would, can you still brag that you love me more than any of these other disciples love me?"

In His mercy (and not unlike a healing exercise), Jesus allowed Peter to reaffirm his love three times. And then He confirmed that Peter would indeed have to lay down his life.

Rejoice:
to feel or show great
happiness or delight.

According to Peter's first New Testament letter, the hard things we experience in this life are *always* eclipsed by the bigger things God is doing in and through them. Which means instead of lamenting our lack, we should be rejoicing in it. "Beloved, do not be surprised at the fiery trial when it comes upon you to test you, as though something strange were happening to you. But rejoice insofar as you share Christ's sufferings, that you may also rejoice and be glad when his glory is revealed" (1 Pet. 4:12–13).

Rejoicing in trials is a lot easier said than done. But the way we respond to suffering will be determined by how well we understand (1) its purpose in our lives, as well as (2) the blessing it holds, because of (3) how radically good God is.

As "exiles scattered," such knowledge is particularly important, which brings us to this Bible study and this reality: followers of Jesus are citizens of heaven, though for now we live here and—yes—we suffer. But like Peter, we have a calling to share the gospel no matter the circumstances. To tell others about the hope we have because our eyes are fixed on heaven and the joy that awaits us there. To make room for God to grow deep roots of strength and faith in our hearts, because our struggles are being eclipsed again and again and again by the goodness of the Lord.

And in His goodness, we rejoice.

"Blessed be the God and Father of our Lord Jesus Christ! According to his great mercy, he has caused us to be born again to a living hope through the resurrection of Jesus Christ from the dead, to an inheritance that is imperishable, undefiled, and unfading, kept in heaven for you, who by God's power are being guarded through faith for a salvation ready to be revealed in the last time."

1 Peter 1:3–5

Lesson 1

Death is eclipsed by

LIFE

EXT. CITRUS GROVE

(Elizabeth hurriedly leads Mary to a small citrus grove nearby. The pair sit, clasping hands, Elizabeth breathless. Young Mary is cooperative but bewildered. Elizabeth closes her eyes and bursts—)

ELIZABETH: Blessed are you among women, and blessed is the fruit of your womb!

YOUNG MARY *(looking again at Elizabeth's bump)*: Wait. How did you know? Ah, I suppose nothing should surprise me anymore.

ELIZABETH *(Elizabeth is overwhelmed, her words coming faster than she can think)*: Something better than that is happening. So humbling. Why is this granted to me that the mother of my Lord should come to me?

YOUNG MARY: Did a messenger tell you about me?

ELIZABETH: When I heard your voice, just the sound of your greeting, my baby leaped for joy. And blessed are you who believed there would be a fulfillment from what was spoken to you from Adonai.

YOUNG MARY: So a messenger did tell you—

ELIZABETH: The messenger came to my husband. Zechariah said, "I don't believe it."

YOUNG MARY *(putting her hand on Elizabeth's)*: May we just slow down a moment? You're not in a condition to be losing your breath *(they breathe together)*. When my

messenger told me about your news, I was so happy, knowing how long you'd suffered …
I want to hear all about it!

ELIZABETH (*chuckling*): The reason Zechariah could not speak with you is that he did not believe the message from God about me.

YOUNG MARY: I wasn't sure at first, either.

ELIZABETH: I feel bad he has to go through this, but I must admit sometimes … (*whispering—*) I don't mind the quiet. But he wrote down for me what was spoken, and I memorized every word: that his name will be John.

YOUNG MARY: Not Zechariah? Why John?

ELIZABETH: Well, perhaps he will not be a priest like his father. A different path for God. For Zech was also told John will turn many of the children of Israel to the Lord their God, and he will go before Him in the spirit and power of Elijah, to turn the hearts of the fathers to the children, and the disobedient to the wisdom of the just, and to make ready for the Lord a people prepared. To prepare the way for … (*she nods at Mary's bump and puts her hand to her own—*) Oh! There he goes again! Feel it!

YOUNG MARY (*laughing with delight*): Yes!

ELIZABETH (*overwhelmed*): It's like he can't wait to get started.

Good News, Bad News

John the Baptist was sent to proclaim the coming Messiah. He was the forerunner (Matt. 3:1–12), preparer of the way (Isa. 40:3), and the one who called people to repentance in order to prepare their hearts for the "Lamb of God, who takes away the sin of the world!" (Mark 1:4; John 1:29–30).

Herald:
an official messenger bringing news; a person or thing viewed as a sign that something is about to happen.

Jesus and the life He offers were coming into the world, and John was the herald of that good news. But, as is sometimes the case, bad news comes along with the good, because in order for our sins to be forgiven, we have to first acknowledge them and repent. In

Repent:
to feel and express sincere regret or remorse about sin.

order for us to follow, we have to abandon the things that offend God. In order to experience the Lord's abundant provision, we have to accept our own pathetic lack. And in order to be "born again to a living hope," we first have to die.

Your Turn

1. Following Jesus requires that we turn away from sin, surrender our future plans, and trust Him to take care of us—and all that on a daily basis. In what ways do you imagine that was hard for John the Baptist's elderly mother? For Jesus's teenage mother? In what ways are those things hard for you?

For Bible Nerds (like us) Who Want to Know

In the Gospel of John, the "Lamb of God" moniker that John the Baptist used for Jesus has a rich history from the Old Testament sacrifice system. In particular, it references the Jewish festival called Passover, which is a remembrance of God's rescuing of the Hebrew people out of slavery to Egypt (called the "Exodus").

In that event, God commanded His people to sacrifice a lamb and smear its blood on their doorframes so God's judgment on Egypt would "pass over" those who demonstrated their allegiance to God (Ex. 12:1–14). In obedience to God's command that they remember His saving work in the Exodus, the Jews continued the annual celebration of Passover with the sacrifice of a lamb.

John the Baptist understood that the symbolism of the Exodus and Passover was coming to its culminating goal, so he identified Jesus as God's provision of a "lamb" who would be sacrificed to save His people from enslavement to sin.

It is no accident that Jesus's death occurred during the Passover festival (see John 18–19). And looking ahead, Jesus is also often referred to as "the Lamb" in the book of Revelation (a book also authored by the apostle John).

Gospel:
the good news
of Jesus Christ.

Survival Instinct

"And calling the crowd to him with his disciples, [Jesus] said to them,
'If anyone would come after me, let him deny himself and take up his
cross and follow me. For whoever would save his life will lose it, but
whoever loses his life for my sake and the gospel's will save it. For what
does it profit a man to gain the whole world and forfeit his soul?'"

Mark 8:34–36

"[John's
followers] came
to John and said
to him, 'Rabbi,
that man who
was with you on
the other side of
the Jordan—the
one you testified
about—look,
he is baptizing,
and everyone is
going to him.' To
this John replied,
'A person can
receive only what
is given them
from heaven.
You yourselves
can testify that
I said, "I am not
the Messiah but
am sent ahead
of him." The
bride belongs to
the bridegroom.
The friend who
attends the
bridegroom
waits and listens
for him, and is
full of joy when
he hears the
bridegroom's
voice. That joy
is mine, and it is
now complete.
He must become
greater; I must
become less.'"
John 3:26–30
(NIV)

Human beings are hardwired to self-protect. Add to that our twenty-
first-century Western culture, which constantly (and almost exclusively)
glorifies self-focus and self-gratification, and you end up with large swaths
of the population actually opposed to God—because you can't put God first
and yourself first at the same time. It's just not possible.

Indeed, we hear "me" messaging on a regular basis. Exhortations to grow
in self-care, self-help, self-worth, self-love. To be proud of being self-made,
self-taught, self-assured, self-determined. To pursue spiritual goals like being
self-affirmed and self-actualized. (Even our phones, which we use for self-
everything, have "I" right in their names!)

In other words, we're strongly encouraged to be self-obsessed.

But while we're busy hyper-focusing on ourselves (and feeling wholly
unsatisfied), Jesus offers an alternative: *die* to yourself—which is quite
a departure from what we're used to. But those of us who follow Jesus must
reject what the world teaches. We have to surrender control and obey God's
Word instead. And in so doing, we render ourselves dead to the "all-powerful"
self and alive to Jesus, giving Him free rein to do what He wills in our lives.

That's what it means to follow. We give up our lives like Jesus gave up
His—and John the Baptist understood the assignment. God tasked him
with preparing the way for the Savior of the world. In fact, it's appropriate
to think of him as the last of the Old Testament–style prophets assigned to
point others to Jesus. Guys like Isaiah, Micah, and Zechariah.

For Bible Nerds (like us) Who Want to Know

SOME OT PROPHECIES AND THEIR FULFILLMENT IN JESUS IN THE NT		
Old Testament	**New Testament**	**Fulfillment**
2 Sam. 7:12–16; Ps. 132:11; Isa. 11:1; Jer. 23:5	Matt. 1:1–17; Luke 3:23–38; John 7:42	The Davidic descent of Christ
Mic. 5:2	Matt. 2:4–6; Luke 2:1–20; John 7:42	The birth of Christ in Bethlehem
Isa. 40:3–5; Mal. 3:1	Matt. 3:1–3; Mark 1:2–4; Luke 3:1–6; 7:24–28; John 1:19–23	John the Baptist as the forerunner of Christ
Mal. 4:5–6	Matt. 11:7–14; 17:10–13; Mark 9:11–13; Luke 1:13–17	John the Baptist as an Elijah-type figure coming before Christ
Isa. 9:1–2	Matt. 4:13–17	Christ's ministry in the region of Galilee
Isa. 29:18–19; 35:5–6; 53:4; 61:1–2	Matt. 8:17; 11:2–6; Luke 4:16–22; 7:18–23	Christ's ministry of miraculous healing and good news
Isa. 42:1–4	Matt. 12:15–21	Christ's compassion in ministry
Deut. 18:15; Isa. 42:1; Ps. 2:7	Luke 9:28–36; Acts 3:19–24; cf. 7:37	Christ as God's provision of one like Moses to speak for Him
Ps. 78:1–4	Matt. 13:34–35	Christ's teaching in parables
Isa. 6:9–10; 53:1	Matt. 13:10–15; Mark 4:10–12; Luke 8:9–10; John 12:37–41	The hard-hearted rejection of Christ's teaching
Isa. 62:11; Zech. 9:9	Matt. 21:1–9; John 12:12–19	Christ's humble entry into Jerusalem on a donkey
Ps. 22:1–18; 34:20; Isa. 52:13–53:12; Zech. 12:10	Matt. 27:32–49; John 19:18–37	Christ's suffering and death on the cross
Ps. 16:8–11; Hos. 6:1–2	Luke 24:46–47; John 2:19–22; Acts 2:22–31	The resurrection of Christ
Ps. 110:1	Matt. 22:41–46; Mark 12:35–37; Luke 20:41–44; Acts 2:32–36	The exaltation of Christ
Joel 2:28–32	Acts 2:1–21, 38–39	Christ's pouring out of the Holy Spirit on believers

"And he began to teach them that the Son of Man must suffer many things and be rejected by the elders and the chief priests and the scribes and be killed, and after three days rise again. And he said this plainly. And Peter took him aside and began to rebuke him. But turning and seeing his disciples, he rebuked Peter and said, 'Get behind me, Satan! For you are not setting your mind on the things of God, but on the things of man.' And calling the crowd to him with his disciples, he said to them, 'If anyone would come after me, let him deny himself and take up his cross and follow me. For whoever would save his life will lose it, but whoever loses his life for my sake and the gospel's will save it. For what does it profit a man to gain the whole world and forfeit his soul?'"

Mark 8:31–36

Once the mission was completed and Jesus came into view, John was expected to pass from the scene. To himself be eclipsed. But the Baptizer didn't cooperate for the sake of obedience alone. Of course, it's good and right to obey God, to follow Jesus no matter the cost, and to trust Him for the outcome—even if that outcome is death. After all, Jesus died and we must die too in order to truly live.

But while the bad news of our "death" is necessary, it's completely overshadowed by the good news that comes right after: we die so that we can be born again to a living hope—which is exactly what the preparer of the way, even in his final hours from a jail cell, was looking toward.

Your Turn

2. Jesus is calling us to follow all the way to the cross. But far too often, we carry our "me first" mentality into our relationship with Him. Meaning, we focus on what He can do for us instead of what we can do for Him. In what ways are you practicing dying to yourself, and in what ways are you still putting yourself first?

3. Read Mark 8:31–36 in the margin above. What name did Jesus call Peter in verse 33(!)? What explanation did He give for such a harsh rebuke?

4. What are "things of God"? What are "things of men"?

Perks of the Job

"Do not lay up for yourselves treasures on earth, where moth and rust destroy
and where thieves break in and steal, but lay up for yourselves treasures in
heaven, where neither moth nor rust destroys and where thieves do not break
in and steal. For where your treasure is, there your heart will be also."

Matthew 6:19–21

The fixation on self is the forfeiture of real treasure. In other words, most of us spend so much time trying to lay up treasure on earth (to feel secure in our bank accounts, be affirmed by others, be as beautiful, smart, or successful as we perceive those around us to be) that we've lost sight of what's already ours in Christ.

In his letter, Peter painted a picture of what followers of Christ have been raised to life *for*: "a living hope" (1 Pet. 1:3). Incidentally, the Bible doesn't teach that we should separate ourselves from all the enjoyment God has provided in the world. While self-control, self-discipline, and even self-sacrifice are praiseworthy Christian virtues (1 Pet. 4:7–11; 2 Pet. 1:3–11), we aren't ascetics. On the contrary, God made the world and everything in it, and He wants us to enjoy what He made within the bounds He intended.

Ascetics: people who punish themselves by denial of basic human needs for some supposed self-earned righteousness.

That said, the reason we've been raised to life is to enjoy Him! Along with all the perks that come from following.

If you're in Christ, you've been "born again to a living hope … to an inheritance that is imperishable, undefiled, and unfading, kept in heaven for you" (1 Pet. 1:3–4). Which means the Creator of the world, the One who set the boundaries for the sea (Jer. 5:22) and owns the cattle on a thousand hills (Ps. 50:10), the author of time and space and galaxies that extend beyond what our telescopes can see (Isa. 40:26), the King whose heavenly throne is encircled by an emerald rainbow (Rev. 4:2–3) along with angelic creatures who worship Him day and night (Rev. 7:11)—

HE has set aside your inheritance.

And there's more. Not only has God stockpiled awesomeness for you in heaven, He's also guarding you on earth. He's protecting, leading, and providing for you in ways you couldn't possibly accomplish on your own, no matter how much me-time you choose to spend. Which begs the question, what need is there for self-preservation when God is willing to do the work for you? How could any one of us do a better job of caring for ourselves than the Lord of life who loves and is love?

Surely His goodness eclipses our "death" and redefines what truly matters in life.

(Spoiler alert, it isn't you.)

Your Turn

5. Christ chose the ultimate suffering so we could be reborn into the hope of His resurrection:

- Life with God on earth where He safeguards every follower for eternity.
- Life with God in heaven where every follower has an inheritance waiting.

How does knowing what you've been saved for make you more willing to die to what you've been saved from?

"Be strong and courageous. Do not fear or be in dread of them, for it is the LORD your God who goes with you. He will not leave you or forsake you."
Deuteronomy 31:6

"The angel of the LORD encamps around those who fear him, and delivers them."
Psalm 34:7

"Fear not, for I am with you; be not dismayed, for I am your God; I will strengthen you, I will help you, I will uphold you with my righteous right hand."
Isaiah 41:10

6. Read the verses in the margin. What are some of the ways God safeguards you on earth?

"'No weapon that is fashioned against you shall succeed, and you shall refute every tongue that rises against you in judgment. This is the heritage of the servants of the LORD and their vindication from me,' declares the Lord."
Isaiah 54:17

"Therefore do not be anxious, saying, 'What shall we eat?' or 'What shall we drink?' or 'What shall we wear?' For the Gentiles seek after all these things, and your heavenly Father knows that you need them all. But seek first the kingdom of God and his righteousness, and all these things will be added to you."
Matthew 6:31–33

7. What does it mean that "where your treasure is, there your heart will be also"? What do you treasure most? What, in Jesus, are you beginning to treasure *more*?

"But the Lord is faithful. He will establish you and guard you against the evil one."
2 Thessalonians 3:3

Our New Reality

"And [John's followers] came to John and said to him, 'Rabbi [Jesus],
who was with you across the Jordan, to whom you bore witness—look,
he is baptizing, and all are going to him.' John answered, 'A person
cannot receive even one thing unless it is given him from heaven. You
yourselves bear me witness, that I said, "I am not the Christ, but I have
been sent before him." The one who has the bride is the bridegroom. The
friend of the bridegroom, who stands and hears him, rejoices greatly at
the bridegroom's voice. Therefore this joy of mine is now complete.
He must increase, but I must decrease.'"

John 3:26–30

Side note:
Dying to sin might sound
like bad news at first, but
we should remember that
it's actually the good news
of being rescued from
enslavement to sin! And
rescue from enslavement
should always be viewed as
good news (see Rom. 6).

Obviously.

Bad news does sometimes tag along with the good, and
for us to be alive in Christ we do have to die to sin. Which
means the only hyphenated words we should have on repeat
are the ones we mentioned before, like self-control, self-
discipline, and self-sacrifice. Or better still, Jesus-focused,
Spirit-controlled, heaven-bound, and hope-filled.

Because we're not the One we need.

On the contrary, we need Jesus. We need the hope His
resurrection provides, the protection His presence promises,
and the satisfaction our souls find only in Him. Oh that we'd
learn to say along with the herald of the good news of the gospel of Jesus Christ:

He must increase. We must decrease.

Your Turn

8. How can you increase your Jesus-focus today?

Seasons 3 and 4 of *The Chosen* include psalms from the Old Testament, which is why each lesson of this study will close with one.

The book of Psalms is a collection of songs, hymns, poetry, and prayers. Some inspire praise, some bring comfort in grief, but all of them can be spoken in prayer when words otherwise fail us.

Prayer Focus

Praise Jesus for dying for your sin, so that you could die to your sin. Praise Him for rising from the dead, so that you could rise to new life too. Thank Him for guarding you in the here and now, and for the inheritance He is setting aside for you in heaven. Ask Him to increase as you follow, and to help you decrease.

Sample Prayer

Preserve me, O God, for in you I take refuge. I say to the LORD, "You are my Lord; I have no good apart from you." As for the saints in the land, they are the excellent ones, in whom is all my delight. The sorrows of those who run after another god shall multiply; their drink offerings of blood I will not pour out or take their names on my lips. The LORD is my chosen portion and my cup; you hold my lot. The lines have fallen for me in pleasant places; indeed, I have a beautiful inheritance. I bless the LORD who gives me counsel; in the night also my heart instructs me. I have set the LORD always before me; because he is at my right hand, I shall not be shaken. Therefore my heart is glad, and my whole being rejoices; my flesh also dwells secure. For you will not abandon my soul to Sheol, or let your holy one see corruption. You make known to me the path of life; in your presence there is fullness of joy; at your right hand are pleasures forevermore.

Psalm 16

EXT. EXECUTION CHAMBER HALLWAY (DAWN)

(In the dim light just before sunrise, Palace Guards flank John the Baptizer. His hands are bound and his shackled feet stumble as the guards pull him.

A heavy wooden door swings open to a large room with stone walls and John sees the chopping block. His face betrays neither shock nor fear.

A soldier polishes a gleaming platter.)

JOHN THE BAPTIZER: That's a nice plate. Silver?

SOLDIER: Only the finest. Intended for a royal wedding banquet, requested by King Herod himself. *(After a beat, John chuckles.)* Why are you laughing?

JOHN THE BAPTIZER: I've never been to a wedding banquet. But I'm on my way to one.

SOLDIER: What's that mean?

JOHN THE BAPTIZER: Oh, never mind. You wouldn't get it.

GUARD WITH CLIPBOARD *(looking up from his inmate termination paperwork)*: Are those your final words? *(Murmuring as he writes—)* You ... wouldn't ... get it.

GUARD WITH CLIPBOARD (CONT'D) *(as the executioner takes his position—)*: John, son of Zechariah and Elizabeth of Judea, here on this day, by order of His Majesty King Herod Antipas ...

(By the time we hear the word "King," the recitation has been reduced to a low, inscrutable mumble. Music rises as John sees something down the hill, in the golden rays of morning light in a small clearing—a lamb. Grazing. Wiggling an ear. Behold ...)

JOHN THE BAPTIZER *(as he smiles and whispers—)*: Thank You ...

"In this you rejoice, though now for a little while, if necessary, you have been grieved by various trials, so that the tested genuineness of your faith—more precious than gold that perishes though it is tested by fire—may be found to result in praise and glory and honor at the revelation of Jesus Christ. Though you have not seen him, you love him. Though you do not now see him, you believe in him and rejoice with joy that is inexpressible and filled with glory, obtaining the outcome of your faith, the salvation of your souls."

1 Peter 1:6–9

Lesson 2

Grief is eclipsed by
PRAISE

INT. MISSION HOUSE—STUDY (MORNING)

(Jesus sits up from a resting mat on the floor of what used to be Matthew's study. The windows are draped in dark cloth, the only light coming from a small oil lamp nearby.)

ANDREW: Rabbi? *(Jesus turns, sees Andrew in the doorway, looking shabby, his shirt torn at the collar. Andrew holds a cup of water and a small plate of food.)*

ANDREW (CONT'D) *(bending down to set the provisions on the floor)*: I'll just, I'll set this here.

JESUS: It's all right. Please come in. Sit with me.

(Andrew joins Him on the floor.)

JESUS (CONT'D): How are you holding up?

ANDREW: I ... I don't exactly know what to say. I thought I would be far worse. Apparently Simon thinks so too. He keeps checking on me every five minutes.

JESUS *(smiling)*: Like how you continue to check on Me?

ANDREW: You knew John longer than any of us. But then You're ...

"In this you rejoice ..."

In **what** do you rejoice?

Context matters. So any time there are phrases or words like "Therefore," "So," or "Now then," you should dig deeper to find out what's being referenced. In this case, Peter is referring to what he just described: "According to his great mercy, he has caused us to be born again to a living hope through the resurrection of Jesus Christ from the dead, to an inheritance that is imperishable, undefiled, and unfading, kept in heaven for you.... *In this you rejoice ...*" You rejoice in being born anew and in the reward that awaits you in heaven.

JESUS: I'm what?

ANDREW: You're ... I mean, You're ...

JESUS: Then why would you need to check on Me?

ANDREW: Okay, well, then I'll just say You're a mystery.

JESUS (*eating a piece of the bread and choking a bit on its dryness*): Oh wow.

ANDREW: I know. It's pretty stale.

JESUS: Pretty? (*He takes a sip to wash it down and both men laugh.*) Tastes like Elijah's bones.

(*They laugh harder.*)

ANDREW: Can we be laughing?

JESUS: Why not? You know, some of the moments in which we laugh the hardest come around the time of a funeral. Our hearts are so tender, all our emotions are right at the surface; laughter and tears closer than ever. And believe me—I sat many a shiva with John when we were kids and he could not hold a sullen mood for seven straight days. Never happened.

> Shiva:
> a period of seven days of formal mourning for the dead, beginning immediately after the funeral; a ritual referred to as "sitting shiva."

ANDREW: I feel guilty. I should be in shambles.

JESUS: No. No, Andrew, there is no *should* in grief. There's no right way to mourn. You already experienced much grief when John was arrested. Falling to pieces again would not honor John's memory any more than feeling nothing at all. Hmm?

JESUS (CONT'D): So, you say I am a mystery?

ANDREW: Well, I-I mean You ...

JESUS: Who did John say I am?

ANDREW: John said... The One.

(*Jesus STANDS and goes to the window. To Andrew's shock, Jesus removes the heavy drape. Harsh daylight pours in.*)

ANDREW (CONT'D): What are You doing?!?

JESUS (*heading for the door—*): You've given Me an idea. Where do we traditionally sit shiva?

ANDREW: The home of the deceased?

JESUS: And where's was John's home?

ANDREW: The open road ...

JESUS: Gather the others.

Precious Faith

Peter said we'd be "grieved by various trials." That's a pretty wide net, but it's accurate because humanity's problems run the gamut. From not having enough money to being responsible for an abundance. From being burdened by the pain of a loved one to feeling loved by no one. From experiencing the consequences of our own sin to becoming the victim of someone else's. From being deficient physically, mentally, or emotionally to our abilities going unnoticed, unutilized, or unappreciated. From unexpected tragedy to the chronic illnesses that seem to steal our years away.

There are just so many reasons to grieve. Yet, somehow, trials purify our faith.

> Run the gamut:
> a saying that means to experience or display the complete range of something.

For Bible Nerds (like us) Who Want to Know

It's easy for us in the twenty-first century to assume belief was easier for the first-century followers of Jesus. They could see Him, hear Him, literally touch Him. It sometimes feels like we're more limited in our access to the evidence of Jesus being real.

Peter wrote with an awareness of the benefit he had in being an eyewitness to Jesus on earth. In his second letter to the churches in Asia Minor, he referred to his experience with James and John on the Mount of Transfiguration and said:

"For we did not follow cleverly devised myths when we made known to you the power and coming of our Lord Jesus Christ, but we were eyewitnesses of his majesty. For when he received honor and glory from God the Father, and the voice was borne to him by the Majestic Glory, 'This is my beloved Son, with whom I am well pleased,' we ourselves heard this very voice borne from heaven, for we were with him on the holy mountain" (2 Pet. 1:16–18; see also Matt. 17:1–8; Mark 9:2–8; Luke 9:28–36).

And so, Peter congratulates his readers for believing without the advantages of physically meeting Jesus.

"Though you have not seen him, you love him. Though you do not now see him, you believe in him and rejoice with joy that is inexpressible and filled with glory" (1 Pet. 1:8–9).

According to Peter, faith in Jesus means we believe Him for what we don't yet see. It means we continually surrender, even when our circumstances are far from ideal. It means we trust Him to provide, even when our bank accounts come up short. It means we remain confident that God's words are true, even when the world says they're not. It means we stand firm knowing He won't fail us. Or leave us. Or forget us.

That kind of radical faith is purified by trials the way gold is purified by fire, which is an appropriate metaphor since the world is going to hell in a handbasket. Seems in order to go the distance with Jesus, we're going to need the kind of faith that does too.

"Dear friends, do not be surprised at the fiery ordeal that has come on you to test you, as though something strange were happening to you. But rejoice inasmuch as you participate in the sufferings of Christ."
1 Peter 4:12–13 (NIV)

Your Turn

1. We don't often think of Jesus being "grieved by various trials," but He was. What kinds of trials do you imagine He grieved? What trials in your life are you grieving?

Trial by Fire

"I will ... refine them as one refines silver, and test them as gold is tested. They will call upon my name, and I will answer them. I will say, 'They are my people'; and they will say, 'The LORD is my God.'"

Zechariah 13:9

Gold is found in ore and is either mined from the ground or collected from alluvial deposits in riverbeds. At first, it's barely discernable among all its impurities. Sand and dirt have to be washed away, and then whatever's left has to be placed into fire. When gold reaches its melting point (1,947° F), it liquifies, separating the pure gold from the impure metals and contaminants it was once inextricably linked to.

That's the process for gold. It's also the process for us. Because in order for our faith to be separated from impurities it's otherwise linked to, we must go through the Refiner's fire.

So, what contaminates our faith? What impurities must be purged? No doubt there are lots of things we could point to, but they can be summarized in one word: unbelief. We don't wholly believe what the Bible says about life and death, right and wrong, truth and goodness, happiness and wholeness, sin and salvation, or what actually matters unto eternity.

In other words, the thing that must be removed from our faith is our lack of faith. Like the process of purifying gold, our sin is washed away (thank You, Jesus) and whatever's left is placed into the proverbial fire. Which means sometimes God allows our circumstances to be far from ideal so that we won't trust in them. He allows our bank accounts to come up short so that we'll look to Him for provision instead. He allows us to be challenged so that when His words prove true, our confidence in Him grows.

We are grieved by various trials so that our faith—more precious than gold—will lead us to hope. And then to praise.

Ore:
natural rock or sediment typically containing metals that can be mined, treated, and sold at a profit.

Alluvial deposits:
loose clay, silt, sand, or gravel that has been carried and placed by running water.

"Behold, I have refined you, but not as silver; I have tried you in the furnace of affliction."
Isaiah 48:10

"The crucible is for silver, and the furnace is for gold, and the LORD tests hearts."
Proverbs 17:3

"But who can endure the day of his coming, and who can stand when he appears? For he is like a refiner's fire ... He will sit as a refiner and purifier of silver, and he will purify the sons of Levi and refine them like gold and silver, and they will bring offerings in righteousness to the LORD."
Malachi 3:2–3

"For to set the mind on the flesh is death, but to set the mind on the Spirit is life and peace."
Romans 8:6

"Thus says the LORD: Do justice and righteousness, and deliver from the hand of the oppressor him who has been robbed. And do no wrong or violence to the resident alien, the fatherless, and the widow, nor shed innocent blood in this place."
Jeremiah 22:3

"These are the things that you shall do: Speak the truth to one another; render in your gates judgments that are true and make for peace; do not devise evil in your hearts against one another, and love no false oath, for all these things I hate, declares the LORD."
Zechariah 8:16–17

"But godliness with contentment is great gain, for we brought nothing into the world, and we cannot take anything out of the world. But if we have food and clothing, with these we will be content. But those who desire to be rich fall into temptation, into a snare, into many senseless and harmful desires that plunge people into ruin and destruction. For the love of money is a root of all kinds of evils. It is through this craving that some have wandered away from the faith and pierced themselves with many pangs."
1 Timothy 6:6–10

Your Turn

2. In what ways are trials testing the genuineness of your faith?

3. Look at the verses in the margins here and above. What does the Bible say about your current circumstances?

4. Read Romans 8:18 and Revelation 21:1–7. In your own words, describe the temporary nature of grief and how it doesn't compare to the eternal outcome of your faith in Jesus Christ.

So That

"Therefore, since we have been justified by faith, we have peace with God through our Lord Jesus Christ. Through him we have also obtained access by faith into this grace in which we stand, and we

rejoice in hope of the glory of God. Not
only that, but we rejoice in our sufferings,
knowing that suffering produces endurance,
and endurance produces character, and
character produces hope, and hope does
not put us to shame, because God's love
has been poured into our hearts through
the Holy Spirit who has been given to us."

Romans 5:1–5

Suffering exposes the things we instinctively hope in, like financial security, physical comfort, other people, our own strength, plans, health, and accomplishments. When any of those things are threatened—and we realize how fragile and futile they actually are—we tend to panic.

But we also tend to pray.

Sometimes we turn to God in anger. Sometimes we turn to Him in tears. Sometimes we turn to God in pure desperation. In any case, we ask hard questions like *Why would You? How could You?* Because suffering seems to automatically bring with it a lot of confusion, hurt, fear, second-guessing, and even judgment of God's character and the things He allows.

But the truth is that God sees beyond the moment we're living in. He knows all the ways our faith is deficient, and how unbelief endangers our ability to keep following. He knows the character qualities we need more of, and He knows exactly when we're going to need them. He knows

"For we ourselves were once foolish, disobedient, led astray, slaves to various passions and pleasures, passing our days in malice and envy, hated by others and hating one another. But when the goodness and loving kindness of God our Savior appeared, he saved us, not because of works done by us in righteousness, but according to his own mercy, by the washing of regeneration and renewal of the Holy Spirit, whom he poured out on us richly through Jesus Christ our Savior, so that being justified by his grace we might become heirs according to the hope of eternal life."
Titus 3:3–7

"But whatever gain I had, I counted as loss for the sake of Christ. Indeed, I count everything as loss because of the surpassing worth of knowing Christ Jesus my Lord. For his sake I have suffered the loss of all things and count them as rubbish, in order that I may gain Christ and be found in him, not having a righteousness of my own that comes from the law, but that which comes through faith in Christ, the righteousness from God that depends on faith— that I may know him and the power of his resurrection, and may share his sufferings, becoming like him in his death, that by any means possible I may attain the resurrection from the dead."
Philippians 3:7–11

Endurance:
your ability to trust God
for longer periods of
time, through greater
degrees of difficulty.

Character:
your true nature that is being
conformed to the image
of Christ (Rom. 8:29–30).

In other words, you are being
fundamentally changed from
the inside out to think and
respond and walk like Jesus.

Hope:
your confident expectation
that God will keep His
promises, in this world
and in the one to come.

the plans He has for us, to prosper and not to harm us, to give us hope and a future (Jer. 29:11).

Which means the Refiner's fire, though painful and grief laden, is part of a master plan to (a) make us more like Jesus and (b) bring us into a closer relationship with Him, so that (c) we'll know the hope to which we've been called. To that end, suffering is allowed so that endurance will increase. Because endurance produces character. And character produces hope.

And hope does not disappoint or put us to shame because it's not a wish; hope is an anticipation of what is surely coming and is already here! We can be confident in God's provision and constant presence on earth because He has proven Himself trustworthy again and again (Matt. 7:7–11). We can be confident in our future with Him in heaven because Jesus conquered the grave and ascended to the place He's now preparing for those who follow Him (John 14:2–6; Luke 24:50–53). And when we follow, all things work together for our good according to His purposes (Rom. 8:28), which means nothing—including grief—can snatch us from His hand (John 10:27–29).

Your Turn

5. How do you typically respond to God in your grief?

6. Read Psalms 34:18; 103:6–14; and 2 Peter 3:9. How does God respond to *you* and your pain, anger, fear, and confusion?

7. Describe the hope (not the mere wish) you have in Jesus.

Defiant Praise

"For this reason I bow my knees before the Father ... so that Christ may dwell in your hearts through faith—that you, being rooted and grounded in love, may have strength to comprehend with all the saints what is the breadth and length and height and depth, and to know the love of Christ that surpasses knowledge, that you may be filled with all the fullness of God. Now to him who is able to do far more abundantly than all that we ask or think, according to the power at work within us, to him be glory in the church and in Christ Jesus throughout all generations, forever and ever. Amen."

Ephesians 3:14–21

When it comes to suffering and the grief it multiples, here's the bottom line: God's love for you along with His intimate knowledge of what you're going through, His assurance to keep and grow you, His promise of future glory where trials and tears will be no more—all these things culminate in the "praise and glory and honor" of our Lord Jesus (1 Pet. 1:7). They just do. Or at least they will eventually, because we can't help it. We're hardwired to praise the Savior, to defy our circumstances with "joy that is inexpressible and filled with glory," because we know that the One who has allowed hard things loves us beyond comprehension.

When we begin to grasp the enormity of His love, we become more willing to accept our trials and grief because we trust Him.

We trust Him.

As Simon Peter said, we're grieved by many trials. But, in spite of them, Peter stood firm because he knew exactly who Jesus was—who He truly *is*—and he praised Him:

"You are the Christ, the Son of the living God" (Matt. 16:13–20).

That kind of radical faith—once tested and purified and made more precious than gold—will indeed keep us defiantly praising all the way to heaven.

Your Turn

8. Reread Ephesians 3:14–21 and list some of the reasons our grief is eclipsed by praise.

Prayer Focus

Praise God for His refining fire and for loving you enough to make you more like Jesus. Thank Him for the patience and forgiveness He continually extends. Ask Him for strength and wisdom as you navigate your trials, and for a greater awareness of His presence and unconditional love.

Sample Prayer

The LORD upholds all who are falling and raises up all who are bowed down. The eyes of all look to you, and you give them their food in due season. You open your hand; you satisfy the desire of every living thing. The LORD is righteous in all his ways and kind in all his works. The LORD is near to all who call on him, to all who call on him in truth. He fulfills the desire of those who fear him; he also hears their cry and saves them. The LORD preserves all who love him, but all the wicked he will destroy. My mouth will speak the praise of the LORD, and let all flesh bless his holy name forever and ever.

Psalm 145:14–21

EXT. CAESAREA PHILIPPI—THE GATES OF HELL

(Jesus and the disciples come to a stop near a dark, foreboding cave in the side of a mountain with water pouring from it—the fountainhead of the Jordan. Jesus turns around, regarding the group with a friendly smile. They are stunned.)

JESUS: Come, come.

SIMON: Rabbi ... this place?

ANDREW: Respectfully, Rabbi, why did You bring us here? It's an abomination.

JESUS: That's a pretty strong word, Andrew.

PHILIP: Rabbi, during shiva?

JESUS: Should we avoid dark places out of fear, or should we be light to them, like Simon and Judas were on their mission? You think my cousin would be afraid of this cave? Do you think he would be so appalled by what happens in that temple over there that he couldn't stand to be in this place?

In ancient Israel, Caesarea at Philippi was the religious center for Baal worship, and it eventually led to the worship of *many* false gods, including Greek gods. For generations, the region was dominated by pagan practices and unspeakable acts of sexual immorality. The city itself was located at the base of a cliff where spring water flowed. The water ran directly out of the mouth of a cave and into the deep waters below. Since the people believed that caves were gateways to the underworld, this particular one came to be known as "The Gates of Hell."

(The disciples look a little sheepish. One by one, they resign and ready themselves to listen. Matthew takes out his notebook.)

JESUS (CONT'D): Who do people say the Son of Man is?

(The disciples trade glances. Who's gonna go first?)

JOHN: Some say ... You are Elijah, the one who preaches repentance.

JESUS: Hmm.

ANDREW: Others say Jeremiah because he was rejected by the leaders of his time.

BIG JAMES: And still others say one of the prophets, those that spoke on God's behalf.

(Pregnant pause. Simon can't hold it in. He addresses the group without fully turning his head around—)

SIMON: Okay, what are we going to have to do, cast lots? Nathanael, this is your moment. Be yourself.

NATHANAEL: Some say John the Baptizer.

(Exhalations of combined frustration and relief tumble out of the group at this sentiment.)

PHILIP: Which obviously isn't true.

JESUS: Okay, well that's everyone else. But who do you say that I am?

SIMON *(staring straight at Jesus, unflinching)*: You are the Christ, the Son of the living God. These carved statues of Baal and Pan and other idols that we passed, they're dead and decaying, but we worship a living God, and You are His Son.

JESUS *(beaming at Simon, His eyes well)*: Blessed are you, Simon, son of Jonah. For flesh and blood has not revealed this to you, but My Father in heaven. All your life you've been called Simon, "One Who Hears," but today, I call you Peter ... "Rock." And it is on this Rock that I will build My church, and the gates of hell shall not prevail against it. This is a place of death, and I brought you here to tell you that death has no power to hold My redeemed people captive. Because I live, you also will live!

"Concerning this salvation, the prophets who prophesied about the grace that was to be yours searched and inquired carefully, inquiring what person or time the Spirit of Christ in them was indicating when he predicted the sufferings of Christ and the subsequent glories. It was revealed to them that they were serving not themselves but you, in the things that have now been announced to you through those who preached the good news to you by the Holy Spirit sent from heaven, things into which angels long to look."

1 Peter 1:10–12

Questions are eclipsed by
RESOLVE

EXT. ROYAL PALACE—COURTYARD

(King David lies face down on the ground in goat-hair sackcloth before an altar of incense. Two Elders of the House stand at a distance behind a pillar with a plate of food and cup of water.)

ELDER 1 *(whispering intensely)*: He has to eat something, he'll die! As if the grief were not enough?

ELDER 2: It's repentance. For the manner in which the child was conceived.

ELDER 1: Three days, maybe four, I understand. But six?? Can a person live without food for six days?

ELDER 2: If anyone can, it would be him. He's probably gone longer when he was on the run from Saul.

ELDER 1: He was a teenager! If the King of Israel starves on our watch, we'll be executed. This regime has slaughtered people for less … *(proceeding toward the King)* Come on!

ELDER 2 *(gently tugging at David's arm)*: Your Majesty, please. Take some nourishment.

DAVID: Has the child been restored?

ELDER 1: Not yet, but the doctor says he is fighting, my lord.

DAVID: Then leave me to my prayers.

ELDER 2: Batsheva needs you. The child needs you.

DAVID: I said leave. What is needed is my repentance.

(NEXT MORNING) INT. ROYAL PALACE—CHILD'S ROOM

(A devastated doctor shakes his head and reverently takes a small blanket, laying it into a crib, covering what's inside. He turns toward Batsheva, who is waiting nearby, attended by handmaidens.)

BATSHEVA: Doctor?

DOCTOR: He's gone, Your Highness.

EXT. ROYAL PALACE—COURTYARD

(An anguished wail comes from inside the palace. David hears it ... and deflates. Grief overtakes him. The Elders look soberly at one another.)

ELDER 2: What are the right words?

ELDER 1: There are none.

DAVID *(gathering himself, there's a clear shift from devastated to resolute)*: I'm ready.

Unanswered Questions

Life is full of unanswered questions, even for faithful followers of Jesus. Indeed, going where Jesus goes and doing what He commands doesn't automatically grant us knowledge—which seems obvious when you think about it. After all, following isn't leading (duh), which means we often don't get to know where we're going or why things are happening.

We don't have the map.

We didn't write the playbook.

And there's nothing new under the sun because the prophets of the Old Testament had questions too, mostly about how the Lord would bring salvation. They longed for change. They wanted relief from their circumstances. They wanted to move from the era of promise to the era of fulfillment (1 Pet. 1:10–12).

But the job of the prophets was to herald the promise of salvation, which would eventually come through the life, suffering, and resurrection of Jesus. They had a role to play in God's greater plan, and they were required to live it out in spite of their unanswered questions.

Incidentally, so are you.

Your Turn

1. God chose David to be king over Israel and called him "a man after my heart." Yet there's no one in the entire Bible who asked more questions of God than David did—which means there's nothing wrong with asking! What are some of your unanswered questions?

> "And when [God] had removed [Saul], he raised up David to be their king, of whom he testified and said, 'I have found in David the son of Jesse a man after my heart, who will do all my will.' Of this man's offspring God has brought to Israel a Savior, Jesus, as he promised."
> Acts 13:22–23

For Bible Nerds (like us) Who Want to Know

In broad terms, the time of the OT Scriptures is thought of as the era of promise, and the time of the NT is thought of as the beginning of the era of fulfillment. This is illustrated in some of Jesus's own statements recorded in the NT.

For example, after His resurrection, Jesus told His followers, "These are my words that I spoke to you while I was still with you, that everything written about me in the Law of Moses and the Prophets and the Psalms must be fulfilled ... Thus it is written, that the Christ should suffer and on the third day rise from the dead, and that repentance for the forgiveness of sins should be proclaimed in his name to all nations, beginning from Jerusalem" (Luke 24:44–47).

The apostle Paul reflected the same thing, writing, "For I delivered to you as of first importance what I also received: that Christ died for our sins in accordance with the Scriptures, that he was buried, that he was raised on the third day in accordance with the Scriptures" (1 Cor. 15:3–4).

In short, what was promised in the OT has begun to be fulfilled in the NT.

Peter's comment about the prophets of old who longed to know more about the coming of Christ (1 Pet. 1:10–12) is reminiscent of when one of them said: "When I, Daniel, had seen the vision, I sought to understand it" (Dan. 8:15). But Peter's words sound even more like something Jesus said: "For truly, I say to you, many prophets and righteous people longed to see what you see, and did not see it, and to hear what you hear, and did not hear it" (Matt. 13:17; Luke 10:24).

Thus the NT shows the beginning of the fulfillment of the OT promises. But Peter goes on to say something about the second coming of Jesus (1 Pet. 1:13), which we are still awaiting—a promise yet to be fulfilled (see some of Jesus's words on this in John 14:1–3). And we have an assigned mission from Jesus while we wait for His second coming (Matt. 28:18–20; Acts 1:6–8), which is why we describe the NT era as the *beginning* of the fulfillment with more yet to come!

For Bible Nerds (like us) Who Want to Know

David, the youngest son of Jesse from the town of Bethlehem, was a musically talented shepherd boy who served ancient Israel's first king, Saul (1 Sam. 16–17). When Saul became disobedient to God, the Lord announced he would be replaced with "a man after [God's] own heart," which turned out to be David (1 Sam. 13:13–14; Acts 13:22). Ultimately, David reigned as king for forty years (ca. 1010–970 BC), and he's remembered as the most beloved king in Israel's history. Indeed, the Messiah is called "the Son of David" with reference to God's promise to put a descendant of David on the eternal throne of God's people (2 Sam. 7:12–16).

David's transition into kingship was fraught with difficulties, the first of which being that Saul was murderously reluctant to turn over the throne (1 Sam. 18–31; 2 Sam. 1–6). David's kingship had its own problems as well (2 Sam. 11–24). Some of David's reflections on those hardships show up in his many songs that are now part of ancient Israel's hymnbook, the book of Psalms. Among the several different genres of psalms (thanksgiving, wisdom, royal, etc.), the largest is laments.

In lament psalms, the psalmist expresses his unhappy emotions (sadness, fear, anger, confusion, worry, etc.) and calls upon God to intervene. Toward their closing, most lament psalms turn in hope to expressing confidence in God and/or praising Him.

Entitled

> "'For my thoughts are not your thoughts, neither are my ways your ways,' declares the LORD. 'As the heavens are higher than the earth, so are my ways higher than your ways and my thoughts than your thoughts.'"
>
> Isaiah 55:8–9 (NIV)

We have a lot of opinions about how life should and shouldn't go. When our circumstances deviate, we can easily become disillusioned with God. And not only do we have questions regarding *why* things went wrong, we have a lot of emotion attached to those questions.

For example, when trials persist, we can easily feel neglected by God. When we experience strife or loss, we might wonder if He truly cares about our pain. When we're burdened and bogged down, we may question if He'll ever relent. When answers don't come quickly, we may think He's abandoned us altogether.

At different times in his life David felt those things too, and in his psalms of lament he didn't pretend to understand. On the contrary, he spoke gut-wrenchingly honest prayers in which he asked God the hard questions.

> My soul is greatly troubled.
> But you, O LORD—how long?
>
> Psalm 6:3

Why, O LORD, do you stand far away?

Why do you hide yourself in times of trouble?

Psalm 10:1

How long, O LORD? Will you forget me forever?

How long will you hide your face from me?

How long must I take counsel in my soul

and have sorrow in my heart all day?

How long shall my enemy be exalted over me?

Psalm 13:1–2

For you are the God in whom I take refuge; why have you rejected me?

Psalm 43:2

There's plenty more where that came from, and we have a lot to learn from the way David prayed. We could start with the fact that God doesn't need our prayers to be "pretty." He doesn't expect us to be well-spoken, or unemotional, or unwavering in our faith because He knows exactly what we're thinking and feeling already (Ps. 139:1–2). He grieves when we grieve (Ps. 34:18). He keeps track of our tears (Ps. 56:8). And He wants us to pour our hearts out to Him in prayer, like David did (Ps. 55:22), and to trust Him with our doubts and worries and wonderings (Phil. 4:6–7).

But that doesn't mean we're entitled to the answers.

Read that again.

We're not entitled to answers.

And David knew it, which is probably why he refused to stay stuck in lament. Instead, he intentionally shifted his focus from his own suffering to God's character, reminding himself again and again of God's goodness, patience, wisdom, love, and power to save. Because waiting for answers doesn't change who God fundamentally is.

In the midst of unanswered questions, David preached the truth to his own heart by praising the One who is above all and knows all and understands the things we don't. Which is why, in the Psalms, there's always a turn.

Your Turn

2. What do you think of David's questions? Have you asked some of the same ones?

3. Take time to read Psalm 139:1–18, Isaiah 46:8–11, and Romans 11:33–36. In light of these verses, what does it mean that God's thoughts and ways are high above your own?

4. According to Psalm 103:8–16, how does God respond to your questions?

Yet You

"My God, my God, why have you forsaken me? Why are you so far from saving me, so far from my cries of anguish? My God, I cry out by day, but you do not answer, and by night, but I find no rest. Yet you are enthroned as the Holy One; you are the one Israel praises. In you our ancestors put their trust; they trusted and you delivered them. To you they cried out and were saved; in you they trusted and were not put to shame."

Psalm 22:1–5 (NIV)

King David pleaded with God for his son to be healed. He fasted and prayed and implored and grieved so desperately and so constantly that his servants worried about his health. But when the child died, David got up, cleaned up, and worshipped the Lord. When his servants asked him to explain, he expressed his great resolve to trust God in spite of his questions (2 Sam. 12:15–23).

David was honest about his questions, feelings, fears, and regrets—but he didn't stay there because he knew that even without immediate answers, God's (a) presence, (b) promises, and (c) praiseworthiness would eclipse his questions. So, he repeatedly turned toward what he knew to be true. He spoke the truth out loud. He cried it and sang it and stood on it and clung to it and waved it like a banner, for his own sake and for those watching him.

He resolved to believe what was true, and so should we.

Presence. No matter our circumstances, God is always with His children. ALWAYS. As followers of Jesus, we're never alone. Never forgotten. Never overlooked. Never neglected.

"The LORD himself goes before you and will be with you; he will never leave you nor forsake you. Do not be afraid; do not be discouraged."

Deuteronomy 31:8 (NIV)

"The eyes of the LORD are toward the righteous and his ears toward their cry.... When the righteous cry for help, the LORD hears and delivers them out of all their troubles. The LORD is near to the brokenhearted and saves the crushed in spirit."

Psalm 34:15–18

"God is our refuge and strength, a very
present help in trouble."
Psalm 46:1

"The LORD is your keeper; the LORD is your shade on your right hand.
The sun shall not strike you by day, nor the moon by night. The LORD will
keep you from all evil; he will keep your life. The LORD will keep your
going out and your coming in from this time forth and forevermore."
Psalm 121:5–8

Promises. No matter what we're facing, the Bible promises that in the end we'll overcome it because Jesus already has. And while we're waiting, God will meet our needs, grant us wisdom generously, and renew our ability and strength to endure.

"They who wait for the LORD shall renew their strength;
they shall mount up with wings like eagles; they shall run
and not be weary; they shall walk and not faint."
Isaiah 40:31

"Therefore do not be anxious, saying, 'What shall we eat?' or 'What shall we
drink?' or 'What shall we wear?' For the Gentiles seek after all these things, and
your heavenly Father knows that you need them all. But seek first the kingdom
of God and his righteousness, and all these things will be added to you."
Matthew 6:31–33

"I [Jesus] have said these things to you, that in me you may have peace. In the
world you will have tribulation. But take heart; I have overcome the world."
John 16:33

"No temptation has overtaken you that is not common to man. God is faithful, and he will not let you be tempted beyond your ability, but with the temptation he will also provide the way of escape, that you may be able to endure it."

1 Corinthians 10:13

"If any of you lacks wisdom, let him ask God, who gives generously to all without reproach, and it will be given him."

James 1:5

Praiseworthy. No matter our feelings, God deserves our attention, devotion, and worship. But far too often we think of ourselves instead—what others have that we don't, what we need and "deserve," how we're going to achieve our worldly goals, how we might attain a greater degree of satisfaction. Meanwhile, the only One who actually deserves anything is waiting patiently for us to turn our attention *away* from ourselves and *toward* Him.

"Because your steadfast love is better than life, my lips will praise you. So I will bless you as long as I live; in your name I will lift up my hands."

Psalm 63:3–4

"Great is the LORD, and greatly to be praised, and his greatness is unsearchable."

Psalm 145:3

"Finally, brothers, whatever is true, whatever is honorable, whatever is just, whatever is pure, whatever is lovely, whatever is commendable, if there is any excellence, if there is anything worthy of praise, think about these things."

Philippians 4:8

"[Jesus] is the radiance of the glory of God and the exact imprint of

his nature, and he upholds the universe by the word of his power.

After making purification for sins, he sat down at the right hand

of the Majesty on high, having become as much superior to angels

as the name he has inherited is more excellent than theirs."

Hebrews 1:3–4

Your Turn

5. How does God's presence eclipse your unanswered questions?

Look back at your answer
to question #1. How do
the verses above (or any
others in the Bible for
that matter) speak to your
unanswered questions?
For example, are you
wanting to know if or
when you'll be healed?
Meditate on Psalm 34:18.
Do you want to know how
on earth you're going
to pay the mortgage
this month? Meditate
on Matthew 6:31–33.
Do you want to know when
you'll experience the fruits of
your hard and arduous labor?
Meditate on Psalm 63:3–4.

6. How do God's promises eclipse your unanswered
questions?

7. How does God's praiseworthiness eclipse your
unanswered questions?

Right Words

"Likewise the Spirit helps us in our weakness. For we do not know what to pray for as we ought, but the Spirit himself intercedes for us with groanings too deep for words. And he who searches hearts knows what is the mind of the Spirit, because the Spirit intercedes for the saints according to the will of God. And we know that for those who love God all things work together for good, for those who are called according to his purpose."

Romans 8:26–28

Truth is, our lack of understanding and wisdom can cause us to ask the wrong questions. But even then, God works on our behalf. According to the New Testament book of Romans, the Holy Spirit—third person of the Trinity—knows *exactly* what to say and He intercedes for us. Which means, He's filling the space between us and the unknown. He's using His knowledge of God's will and our own hearts to intervene on our behalf. He's focused on glorifying Jesus and making us like Him (John 14:26), while He keeps our name and unique circumstances ever before the throne of God.

Such knowledge should increase our resolve to trust, even when our questions go unanswered. Like the prophets who came before us—those who stood fast and remained faithful for their sake *and* ours—we can resolve to believe God will bring about His perfect plan in His perfect time.

For Bible Nerds (like us) Who Want to Know

Trinity = the state of being three.

"God is a Trinity, Father, Son, and Holy Spirit, each an uncreated person, one in essence, equal in power and glory" (Evangelical Theological Society).

Common analogies include an egg, which has three distinct parts (shell, white, yolk) but remains one egg, or an apple, which has three distinct parts (skin, flesh, core) but remains one apple.

Of course, all analogies eventually break down, and God is not an egg or an apple. Duh.

Each member of the Trinity is not a "part" of God; each is fully God. So while we can define the word in the best possible human terms, the Trinity is a concept we won't fully understand until we're in heaven.

Your Turn

8. Meditate on the fact that the Holy Spirit is interceding for *you*. How does that knowledge change the way you wait for God to answer your questions or change your circumstances?

Sample Prayer

How long, O LORD? Will you forget me forever? How long will you hide your face from me? How long must I take counsel in my soul and have sorrow in my heart all the day? How long shall my enemy be exalted over me? Consider and answer me, O LORD my God; light up my eyes, lest I sleep the sleep of death, lest my enemy say, "I have prevailed over him," lest my foes rejoice because I am shaken. But I have trusted in your steadfast love; my heart shall rejoice in your salvation. I will sing to the LORD, because he has dealt bountifully with me.

Psalm 13

The turn!

Prayer Focus

Praise God for His greatness, His steadfast love, His power to uphold the universe itself, and that He prays for you. Ask Him your questions—be honest and vulnerable and expectant. Ask for strength and faith to trust Him while you wait for answers, but also acknowledge that His wisdom and ways are far above your own.

INT. ROYAL PALACE—PRIVATE CHAMBERS

(David dresses while Batsheva sits nearby.)

BATSHEVA: Why are we getting ready for a dinner I cannot eat? How can you eat at a time like this?

DAVID: While the child was still alive, I fasted and wept.

BATSHEVA: As you should be now.

DAVID: Would that bring him back again? I asked of our God whether He might be gracious to us and let our child live ... my prayer was not answered.

BATSHEVA: Why not? Why some prayers and not others?

DAVID: I don't know. I've never known.

BATSHEVA: And still you worship.

DAVID: I do. Through sorrow and joy. And sorrow again. This *is* the meaning of faith.

BATSHEVA: That cannot bring our son back!

DAVID: No, we can't. But sooner or later we will both go to the same end. He will not return to us, but we will go to him.

BATSHEVA *(beginning to feel strangely comforted)*: The separation is just for now, for a time.

DAVID: A time. It could be a long time; it could be tomorrow. This is the way of all things.

"Therefore, preparing your minds for action, and being sober-minded, set your hope fully on the grace that will be brought to you at the revelation of Jesus Christ. As obedient children, do not be conformed to the passions of your former ignorance, but as he who called you is holy, you also be holy in all your conduct, since it is written, 'You shall be holy, for I am holy.'"

1 Peter 1:13–16

Lesson 4

Confusion is eclipsed by

GRACE

ROAD TO TEL DOR

(Slow-motion. Jesus walks far ahead, trailed at a distance by Thomas and Peter walking alongside the cart holding Ramah's body, wrapped in linen and spices in a box under a heavy drape. The cart is pulled by a donkey led by Zee. The remaining disciples, plus Tamar and Magdalene, and Barnaby and Shula, trail behind. We push in on Simon.)

FLASHBACK TO CAPERNAUM OUTSKIRTS

(Shortly after the murder. The disciples and women are scattered, in shock and comforting each other. Magdalene and Tamar are sitting, faces forlorn. Peter looks at all of them, clearly wondering what to do. He watches as Thomas paces, broken and in shock. Jesus approaches and stands next to him. A pause, then ...)

PETER: I want to do something. I want to help him.

JESUS: You know that's not how grief works.

PETER: I'm failing.

JESUS: Failing at what? This is not a test.

PETER: Being ... You know.

JESUS: I don't.

PETER (*pained*): Who I'm supposed to be now. How can I be a rock for someone in a moment like this?

JESUS: Thomas doesn't need you to be a rock right now.

PETER: He needs a firm footing to walk on. Everything just pulled out from under him.

JESUS: It's the way of all the earth. For now.

PETER: Loss??

JESUS: You know the truth.

PETER: I can't just tell him this is the way of all the earth!

JESUS: Then maybe don't say anything at all. Would words from Thomas have helped after you found out about Eden and the baby? (*This knocks Peter into sober realization. He shakes his head "no."*)

JESUS (CONT'D): You have experienced loss. That makes you more able to go and simply be there with him rather than being the rock.

(*Peter holds a moment, then walks to Thomas. As he approaches, Thomas is still manically pacing.*)

THOMAS: What just happened? I don't even know what just happened.

PETER: I'm so sorry.

THOMAS (*barely breathing*): She's gone, she's gone, she's gone.

PETER: I know. Just breathe.

THOMAS: I can't. I can't breathe, I'm gonna be sick.

PETER (*moving toward Thomas*): Lie back.

(*Thomas falls to his back on the grass. Peter puts his hand on Thomas's shoulder.*)

PETER (CONT'D): What can I do?

(*Thomas shakes his head but grips Peter's hand.*)

Ignorance Isn't Bliss

When it comes to following Jesus and the trials therein, we can easily find ourselves in a whirlwind of confusion. And confusion isn't merely a lack of information, or the conflict between expectations and reality; confusion actually has the potential to turn into profound disappointment. It knocks us off balance. It makes us feel stuck. It steals our joy. It weakens our confidence.

It threatens our faith.

Confusion can, in fact, be paralyzing, because when the ground beneath our feet shifts, our instinct is to self-protect. To hunker down. To retreat from God and sometimes other people. Which means confusion can cause us to lose some of our gospel-sharing boldness and brightness, because when we feel uncertain, it's a lot harder to encourage and spur on the people around us.

But as we discussed in the previous lesson, we're a part of a bigger thing God is doing. And just like the believers who came before us, we can resolve to remain. We can fix our eyes

For Bible Nerds (like us) Who Want to Know

For the early disciples, confusion came with the job, especially when Jesus spoke of His imminent departure and the suffering He would endure at the hands of Jewish authorities. He said:

1. "The Son of Man must suffer many things and be rejected by the elders and chief priests and scribes, and be killed, and on the third day be raised" (Luke 9:22; see also Matt. 16:21–23; Mark 8:31–33).

2. "Let these words sink into your ears: The Son of Man is about to be delivered into the hands of men" (Luke 9:44; see also Matt. 17:22–23; Mark 9:30–32).

3. "See, we are going up to Jerusalem, and everything that is written about the Son of Man by the prophets will be accomplished. For he will be delivered over to the Gentiles and will be mocked and shamefully treated and spit upon. And after flogging him, they will kill him, and on the third day he will rise" (Luke 18:31–33; see also Matt. 20:17–19; Mark 10:32–34).

Reading these things today, it all makes sense; we know the whole story. But for first-century followers—especially those looking to be saved from Rome—Jesus's words didn't sound like predictions of success. The Israelites wanted to be delivered *from* their oppressors, not delivered over to them. And even when Jesus promised that after suffering He would "on the third day be raised"—what did that even mean? No one had ever done anything like it before.

It was too much for the disciples to grasp, and twice in his gospel, Luke explained their confusion: "But they did not understand this saying, and it was concealed from them, so that they might not perceive it. And they were afraid to ask him about this saying" (Luke 9:45) and "But they understood none of these things. This saying was hidden from them, and they did not grasp what was said" (Luke 18:34).

on God's character and His promises. We can choose to praise Him based on who He is instead of how we feel.

We can set our hope on grace.

Your Turn

Confusion:
the state of being
bewildered, uncertain,
conflicted; having disordered
or jumbled thoughts.

followers of Jesus spent a lot of time feeling confused and even ... Jesus was saying and doing. Or *not* doing. But how is confusion ...ent? How does confusion sometimes *lead* to disappointment?

Thorns and Such

"So to keep me from becoming conceited ... a thorn was given me in the flesh, a messenger of Satan to harass me, to keep me from becoming conceited. Three times I pleaded with the Lord about this, that it should leave me. But he said to me, 'My grace is sufficient for you, for my power is made perfect in weakness.' Therefore I will boast all the more gladly of my weaknesses, so that the power of Christ may rest upon me. For the sake of Christ, then, I am content with weaknesses, insults, hardships, persecutions, and calamities. For when I am weak, then I am strong."

2 Corinthians 12:7–10

Throughout his ministry, Paul (author of 2 Corinthians, along with a dozen other books in the New Testament) struggled with something so difficult, he referred to it as "a messenger of Satan." Perhaps he was referring to an actual demon. Perhaps a physical ailment. Perhaps a thought, emotion, or memory he just couldn't shake. Perhaps a combination of all of the above.

There's been endless speculation regarding Paul's thorn. But knowing the precise details doesn't really matter. What matters is that Paul responded to his confusion and frustration by leaning into God's grace.

Sometimes we think "grace" means God will grant us whatever we long for. But clearly in Paul's case, it meant the opposite. In fact, the hardship he faced was the catalyst for God's grace in his life, as well as the conduit through which it continually flowed—from God to Paul, and then from Paul to other people.

On the surface, it seems strange that God's power is made perfect in weakness. In hardships. In suffering. In confusion. But when you really think about it, it makes sense because all those things help get us out of the way. Meaning, when we're weak, we can't meet our own needs, let alone those of others. And our neediness forces us to look to the One who

"Is made perfect" = "My grace is all you need" = "My power accomplishes its purpose when My people fully depend on Me"

For Bible Nerds (like us) Who Want to Know

The significant Christian leader known primarily by his Roman name Paul (formerly known by his Jewish name, Saul) was a first-century Jew and a Roman citizen from Tarsus, the capital of the Roman province of Cilicia (a region in modern Turkey). He was a Pharisee trained in Jerusalem by Gamaliel (Acts 22:3; 23:6; 26:4–5; Phil. 3:5), and he was passionately against Christianity, so much so that he was in favor of hunting down and punishing followers of Jesus (Acts 8:3; 9:1–3; 22:4–5; Gal. 1:13–14; Phil. 3:6).

But that all changed when he met the risen Jesus Christ on the road to Damascus (Acts 9:1–22; cf. Acts 22:1–21; 26:1–32). The former opponent of the Christian faith became a passionate representative of the gospel, traveling around the ancient world preaching the risen Jesus and establishing churches (Acts 13–21). He authored thirteen letters that have been preserved as Scripture among the other New Testament documents.

The former persecutor of Christians ended up being persecuted himself for his faith in Christ (Acts 21–28), and while the New Testament does not record when and how Paul died, early church traditions report that he was beheaded in Rome at the command of Emperor Nero (ca. AD 64–68).

can meet needs—which means confusion is an opportunity to look to God, what He's doing, what He will do, and what He says is surely coming.

Your Turn

2. Describe why Paul might've been confused by his circumstances, but why he was able to simultaneously boast in his weaknesses.

3. What in your own life is confusing for you right now?

4. While confusion has the potential to throw us off balance, according to 2 Corinthians 9:8, what can we be certain of?

State of Grace

"And God is able to make all grace abound to you, so that having all sufficiency in all things at all times, you may abound in every good work."

2 Corinthians 9:8

God is gracious and full of grace. It's fundamental to who He is, which means His grace toward us doesn't ebb and flow. It's not available sporadically or conditionally. On the contrary, God is love (1 John 4:8) and extends grace constantly, even when we don't recognize it. Whether through Christ's death, resurrection, and the resulting free gift of salvation; or through the conviction of sin in order to get our attention; or through the ongoing empowering of the saints to live and act according to their calling. God is always and forever extending grace in spite of any confusion or doubt you may struggle with.

More than that, He's making "all grace abound to you."

Think about that: God is sparing you no good thing. He may not alleviate your suffering when you want Him to. For reasons known only to Him who is all-wise and all-knowing, He may not answer your questions or remove your confusion right away. But He's providing every good thing you need, in every moment of need, so that you'll abound in every good work that He has lovingly planned for you from the dawn of time.

By setting your hope on that extraordinary grace (1 Pet. 1:13), you allow God to work in and through you to change your thoughts and behavior. Thus, focusing on grace leads to sober-minded, obedient living. It makes you ready for action, ready to be utilized by the One who's working to grow His heavenly kingdom until Christ returns (Matt. 16:18–19; 24:42–44). And it allows you to experience confusion without being derailed by it, because God's grace and kindness toward you is a banner of love over everything else (Eph. 3:17–19).

Indeed, God's glorious grace eclipses our temporary confusion. It's not even a fair fight.

Saint:
a person who has been forgiven and made clean by Jesus, and consequently set apart for God's special purposes.

"The LORD is merciful and gracious, slow to anger and abounding in steadfast love."
Psalm 103:8

"And my God will supply every need of yours according to his riches in glory in Christ Jesus."
Philippians 4:19

"Your Father knows what you need before you ask him."
Matthew 6:8

"For I know the plans I have for you, declares the LORD, plans for welfare and not for evil, to give you a future and a hope."
Jeremiah 29:11

Your Turn

5. Describe God's grace in your own words.

6. What does "having all sufficiency in all things at all times" (2 Cor. 9:8) mean for you and any confusion you might currently be grappling with?

7. How does setting your hope on that grace change the way you feel about your circumstances?

Perfect, Not Perfect

"For those who live according to the flesh set their minds on the things of the flesh, but those who live according to the Spirit set their minds on the things of the Spirit. For to set the mind on the flesh is death, but to set the mind on the Spirit is life and peace."

Romans 8:5–6

Peter warned us to not be "conformed to the passions of [our] former ignorance, but as he who called you is holy, you also be holy in all your conduct, since it is written, 'You shall be holy, for I am holy'" (1 Pet. 1:14–16).

Um, what now? It's one thing to set our minds on God's grace and on our confident expectation that Jesus will return and bring our confusion and suffering to an end. But to be perfect as God is perfect? That's an impossibly high, *perhaps even confusing*, standard.

(See what we did there?)

But Peter wasn't saying that we'd be able to attain perfection on earth (and Simon Peter's life as recorded in the New Testament is evidence of that!). He was exhorting us to focus on God's grace to us in Jesus, the only One who has ever lived perfectly holy (1 Pet. 2:22; 1 John 3:5). And by that grace, (a) we have Jesus's righteousness applied to us and (b) we are given the Holy Spirit, who is transforming us, which (c) will reach its pinnacle at the second coming of Jesus.

So, for now, we set our minds on the things of the Spirit. In so doing, we prepare ourselves for action and remain sober-minded because our eyes are fixed on the grace that will surely be poured out and brought to completion when Jesus Christ comes again.

And our confusion becomes much smaller in the shadow of God's overwhelming grace.

"Since then we have a great high priest who has passed through the heavens, Jesus, the Son of God, let us hold fast our confession. For we do not have a high priest who is unable to sympathize with our weaknesses, but one who in every respect has been tempted as we are, yet without sin. Let us then with confidence draw near to the throne of grace, that we may receive mercy and find grace to help in time of need."
Hebrews 4:14–16

Your Turn

8. How does setting your mind on things of the Spirit eclipse confusion, bringing life and peace?

Prayer Focus

Sample Prayer

Incline your ear, O LORD, and
answer me, for I am poor and needy.
Preserve my life, for I am godly; save your
servant, who trusts in you—you are my God. Be
gracious to me, O Lord, for to you do I cry all the day.
Gladden the soul of your servant, for to you, O Lord, do
I lift up my soul. For you, O Lord, are good and forgiving,
abounding in steadfast love to all who call upon you. Give ear,
O LORD, to my prayer; listen to my plea for grace. In the day of
my trouble I call upon you, for you answer me. There is none
like you among the gods, O Lord, nor are there any works like
yours. All the nations you have made shall come and worship
before you, O Lord, and shall glorify your name. For you are
great and do wondrous things; you alone are God. Teach
me your way, O LORD, that I may walk in your truth;
unite my heart to fear your name. I give thanks to
you, O Lord my God, with my whole heart,
and I will glorify your name forever.

Psalm 86:1–12

Praise God for His grace that has accomplished salvation, convicts sinners of sin, and constantly and unconditionally flows in and through His followers. Thank Him for being patient with you. Tell Him what you're still confused by and ask Him to provide the right amount of understanding in His perfect timing. Pray for the strength and resolve you'll need to set your hope fully on the grace that will be brought to you at the revelation of Jesus Christ.

PETER'S HOUSE (NIGHT)

JOHN: Someone should be with Thomas.

PETER: No, he needs to be alone right now.

JOHN: How can you be sure?

PETER: Believe me.

BIG JAMES: What I'm about to say I can only say in front of you two. It's been rattling around in my head all day.

PETER: Careful, James ...

BIG JAMES: Why didn't Jesus do the thing He did with Jairus's daughter??

JOHN (*erupting in a whisper-scream*): I was thinking the exact same thing!! A single word from Him, and we wouldn't be here.

PETER: Boys, we vowed never to speak of what we saw in that house.

BIG JAMES: To anyone else. We know what we saw.

PETER: I understand where you're coming from; I wrestled with exactly the same question about Eden—why He didn't intervene ... I resented His miracles for others.

JOHN: Seems like a reasonable response to me.

PETER: Just remember the words of Isaiah: "'For my thoughts are not your thoughts, neither are my ways your ways,' declares the Lord."

PETER AND JOHN: "For as the heavens are higher than the earth, so are my ways higher than your ways ...

PETER, JAMES, AND JOHN: ... and my thoughts than your thoughts."

BIG JAMES: That doesn't make this easier.

PETER: Jesus had a reason for allowing what happened to Eden that I didn't understand at the time. I may never fully in this lifetime, but I do know it made me desperate for Him.

JOHN: Thomas wasn't inside Jairus's house. He doesn't know for certain that Jesus even *can* bring someone back from death.

BIG JAMES: But he believes Jesus can do anything—and why shouldn't he? And was Jairus's daughter more important than Ramah?

JOHN: Than your unborn child??

PETER: Enough! We told Jesus we'd keep it a secret, and now more than ever it's clear why Thomas must never find out.

JOHN: What if Jesus does it again, but for someone else?

BIG JAMES: It will destroy Thomas.

PETER: Let's just take this one day at a time, all right? Also, we are His students, not His equals.

JOHN: I never said we were equa—

PETER: I mean if we don't know the answer to something, we can let Jesus speak for Himself. You'll write it down. Matthew will write it down. Time will reveal the wisdom hidden in these mysteries. But I trust in the God who walks on water.

"And if you call on him as
Father who judges impartially
according to each one's deeds, conduct
yourselves with fear throughout the time of
your exile, knowing that you were ransomed from
the futile ways inherited from your forefathers, not
with perishable things such as silver or gold, but with the
precious blood of Christ, like that of a lamb without blemish
or spot. He was foreknown before the foundation of the
world but was made manifest in the last times for the
sake of you who through him are believers in God,
who raised him from the dead and gave him glory,
so that your faith and hope are in God."

1 Peter 1:17–21

Lesson 5

Temporal things are eclipsed by
ETERNAL THINGS

ROAD TO BETHANY (MORNING)

(The disciples make their way toward Bethany. Nearing a fork in the road, the group sees eight Roman legionnaires and their leader, a Decanus, approaching the intersection.)

DECANUS: Halt, Jewish citizens!

JESUS *(feeling Big James activate)*: Everyone remain calm.

DECANUS: Disarm yourselves and put down your bags. You're carrying ours now.

TAMAR: WHAT??

MATTHEW: Under Roman law, a soldier can force a Jew to carry his things.

TAMAR: At random??

MATTHEW: There is a legal limit. Maximum of one mile and no further.

PETER: Master, this is humiliating.

JESUS: We will comply. With dignity.

(The soldiers load the disciples down with tents, bronze cooking pots, canteens, flasks, packages of food rations, swords, and heavy shields. One of them fixes his eyes on John.)

Decanus: "chief of ten"; a leader in the Roman army who presided over the eight soldiers and two servants in his assigned squad.

LEGIONNAIRE 1 (*removing his helmet and running his hands through his sweaty hair*): What must it be like, walking around all day with no metal weighing your head down? Ever have helmet hair?

(*He plops his helmet on John's head.*)

LEGIONNAIRE 1 (CONT'D): There.

(*The soldiers immediately laugh at John's expense while muted sounds of shock ripple through the disciples. The other eight Romans do the same thing, depositing their helmets onto the disciples while jeering and mocking. Each Jew cringes with shame or closes his eyes, fuming and devastated as their heads are adorned with the trappings of the Empire. Even Jesus gets one. A soldier shoves a bag of tent poles into Magdalene's chest.*)

LEGIONNAIRE 2: You too.

(*The soldier moves on, but Matthew leans in to take the bag, in addition to his own outsized burden.*)

MATTHEW: I'll take that!

MAGDALENE: I'm not made of straw, Matthew. I can carry it.

MATTHEW (*taking it from her*): Mary, please—I've got it.

DECANUS: Hurry along, rats!

LEGIONNAIRE 1: Rats with nice hats.

(*The disciples trudge forward. Judas is not okay with Jesus taking this on so readily. He tries to remove the helmet from Jesus's head.*)

JUDAS: Master, let me take that; You should not have to—

JESUS: No. No. It is no more unsuitable on My head than any of yours.

JUDAS: We both know that's not true.

JESUS: Thank you for your concern, Judas.

(*Judas is at a loss for words.*)

Futile

We humans have a strong tendency to focus on the wrong things. Things that change and fade and rot and vanish over time. Things like beauty, adoration, respect, reputation, accomplishment, and of course, money. But the truth is, even gold and silver will perish because the things of this world are not going with us into heaven.

Of course, eternity is difficult to wrap our brains around. After all, we live in the here and now. We have people in our lives who we love and are responsible for. We have bills to pay and obligations to meet. We have ideas and goals, and some of us will have the better part of a century to try reaching them. And all that means we can't—and shouldn't—simply check out, no matter how heavenly minded we become.

Nevertheless, Peter reminded his readers that we don't actually belong here. That we're exiles because the moment any one of us chooses to follow Jesus, we become citizens of heaven. This world is no longer our home, so it's actually nonsensical to store up treasure and to strive for what we know won't last.

"[Jesus] came and preached peace to you who were far off and peace to those who were near. For through him we both have access in one Spirit to the Father. So then you are no longer strangers and aliens, but you are fellow citizens with the saints and members of the household of God, built on the foundation of the apostles and prophets, Christ Jesus himself being the cornerstone, in whom the whole structure, being joined together, grows into a holy temple in the Lord. In him you also are being built together into a dwelling place for God by the Spirit."
Ephesians 2:17–22

Think about it. If you were visiting a foreign country and were told customs wasn't going to let you bring anything back, would you spend your time buying souvenirs? Of course not, because there would be far better ways to spend your time and treasure.

The same is true for us. And since the Father judges "according to each one's deeds," it's in our best interest to invest in what actually matters to Him.

Your Turn

1. Like us, the disciples wanted respect, status, security, and stability. But, as we've been discussing, those things don't matter unto eternity. What are some futile things of this world you're currently investing in, and how?

According to Deeds

"Now if anyone builds on the foundation with gold, silver, precious stones, wood, hay, straw—each one's work will become manifest, for the Day will disclose it, because it will be revealed by fire, and the fire will test what sort of work each one has done. If the work that anyone has built on the foundation survives, he will receive a reward. If anyone's work is burned up, he will suffer loss, though he himself will be saved, but only as through fire."

1 Corinthians 3:12–15

Commendation: an award involving special praise.

"[The Lord Jesus] will bring to light the things now hidden in darkness and will disclose the purposes of the heart. Then each one will receive his commendation from God."

1 Corinthians 4:5

"For we must all appear before the judgment seat of Christ, so that each one may receive what is due for what he has done in the body, whether good or evil."

2 Corinthians 5:10

"Blessed is the man who remains steadfast under trial, for when he has stood the test he will receive the crown of life, which God has promised to those who love him."

James 1:12

"Behold, I am coming soon, bringing my recompense with me, to repay each one for what he has done."

Revelation 22:12

Recompense:
to return in kind; to reward good and to punish evil.

Impute:
to ascribe to someone the blessing or debt of another. For the follower of Jesus, our sin was imputed to Christ and His righteousness was imputed to us.

According to Scripture, the day is coming when every person will have to stand before the judgment seat of Christ. Of course, followers of Jesus will not be judged on the basis of sin because God has forgiven our sin and imputed to us the righteousness of Christ. Which means (a) our salvation is secure (John 10:27–29) and (b) God "remembers our sin no more" (Heb. 8:10–12). Rather, our deeds will be judged.

For Bible Nerds (like us) Who Want to Know

In 1 Peter 5:4, the apostle used the word for "crown" that was affiliated with athletic contests: "And when the chief Shepherd appears, you will receive *the unfading crown of glory*." Of course, he's not referring to a literal headpiece; rather, he's talking about the honor due to faithful church leaders that will be given when Jesus returns (1 Pet. 5:1–11).

Paul also used the athletic term to describe people as his "crown" when Jesus comes again: "Therefore, my brothers, whom I love and long for, my joy and *crown*, stand firm thus in the Lord, my beloved" (Phil. 4:1); and, "For what is our hope or joy or *crown* of boasting before our Lord Jesus at his coming? Is it not you?" (1 Thess. 2:19).

Likewise, James 1:12 used the athletic crown term to reference eternal life for those who persevere in faith: "Blessed is the man who remains steadfast under trial, for when he has stood the test he will receive *the crown of life*, which God has promised to those who love him."

The term was used yet again by John to address the subject of life in eternity: "Be faithful unto death, and I will give you *the crown of life*. He who has an ear, let him hear what the Spirit says to the churches. The one who conquers will not be hurt by the second death" (Rev. 2:10–11).

And all that means we shouldn't expect "the crown of life" to be a headpiece worn in heaven. Rather, eternal life with Jesus is itself the reward of persevering faith.

Specifically, our motives and actions and what we did or didn't do for the Lord in the time we were given.

Such knowledge should change what we're choosing, right? It should compel us to do more for the kingdom of God; to be more engaged in His agenda and far less focused on our own; to open our eyes to the needs of others while no longer trying to please them; to become singularly focused on pleasing the One who deserves our praise and who we'll soon see face-to-face—and then be judged by.

(Cue very deep breath.)

Thing is, God knows we humans are motivated by being rewarded, and He uses that desire to keep us focused on investing in *His* kingdom and *His* priorities. To that end, we should wholeheartedly embrace our status as exiles and live like our Father in heaven, who has promised us abundance, beauty, security, and riches beyond our comprehension: "What no eye has seen, nor ear heard, nor the heart of man imagined, what God has prepared for those who love him" (Isa. 64:4; 1 Cor. 2:9).

After all, who wouldn't want a larger stockpile?

Your Turn

2. What emotions arise when you read verses about the judgment seat of Christ, and why?

3. What are some eternal things you could be investing in right now?

4. What awesomeness do you imagine when you think of heaven?
(Reminder: It's even better than that.)

Proper Fear

"The fear of the LORD leads to life, and whoever has it
rests satisfied; he will not be visited by harm."

Proverbs 19:23

God has proven His love for us, that's for sure (Rom. 5:8), and the Bible tells us to rest in His love (Matt. 11:28–30), because we're saved by grace and not by our works (Eph. 2:8–9). The work of salvation has been accomplished (Col. 2:9–15), God keeps watch over our coming and going (Ps. 121:5–8), and He has promised to faithfully meet our needs (Phil. 4:19). Our eternal home is forever secure (John 5:24; 14:2–3), and God is storing up treasure for us there, "where neither moth nor rust destroys and where thieves do not break in and steal" (Matt. 6:19–21).

But God's generosity, kindness, and favor toward us doesn't mean He approves of or even tolerates all our choices. On the contrary, He is in the process of conforming us to the image of His Son (Rom. 8:28–30). As children of God, we're expected to surrender to and obey Him while we're waiting for eternity to commence. When it does, the same One who saved us and cares for us now will judge us (Acts 10:34–43). The One who, as Peter described, "was foreknown before the foundation of the world but was made manifest in the last times" (1 Pet. 1:20).

And that should send a proper chill down our spines. God will judge our works, so we should live with a healthy amount of fear. Not dread or terror or panic, but a solemn understanding that God is watching, that He has promised to discipline us the way a good parent should (Heb. 12:4–11), and that He will hold us accountable for our choices.

So, when Jesus taught His followers to forgive without limits (Matt. 18:21–35) and love even our enemies (5:43–45), when He said things like "if anyone slaps you on the right cheek, turn to him the other also" (v. 39) and "if anyone forces you to go one mile, go with him two miles" (v. 41), He was giving us a picture of who God is. He was helping us understand how God responds. He was explaining how we as God's children are supposed to respond. To choose humility over pride, generosity over materialism, kindness and patience and graciousness over selfishness. To behave in a way that allows people around us to see Jesus in us.

Those of us who believe Him will choose His values over worldly things because (a) our reward in heaven will be great but also because (b) our life on earth will be blessed.

Your Turn

5. Do you believe God loves you in the way it's described above? Why, or why not?

6. Do you fear the Lord in the way it's described above? Why, or why not?

7. According to Galatians 5:22–23, what are some character qualities God cares about and cultivates in the hearts of believers?

Blessed Are

"And he opened his mouth and taught them, saying: 'Blessed are the poor in spirit, for theirs is the kingdom of heaven. Blessed are those who mourn, for they shall be comforted. Blessed are the meek, for they shall inherit the earth. Blessed are those who hunger and thirst for righteousness, for they shall be satisfied. Blessed are the merciful, for they shall receive mercy. Blessed are the pure in heart, for they shall see God. Blessed are the peacemakers, for they shall be called sons of God. Blessed are those who are persecuted for righteousness' sake, for theirs is the kingdom of heaven. Blessed are you when others revile you and persecute you and utter all kinds of evil against you falsely on my account. Rejoice and be glad, for your reward is great in heaven, for so they persecuted the prophets who were before you.'"

Matthew 5:2–12

Blessed is both a familiar and unfamiliar word. Christians tend to use it in place of the word *lucky*, lest anyone think that *we think* good things happen by chance. We also "bless this food to our bodies" before eating, mind our manners with a "bless you" after someone sneezes, give our blessing to things we like and withhold it from things

Throwback to our season 2 Bible study when we spent time learning that "Blessed are the Chosen."

Quid pro quo: a well-known Latin phrase meaning "something for something"; an exchange of favors, as in "you do this thing for me, and then I will do that other thing for you."

we don't, and believe our judgment is subtle when we say, "Bless his heart"—especially if we use a southern drawl.

But when Jesus preached His famous Sermon on the Mount, it's clear the "blessed" statements were not some kind of "do this and be happy" list of life hacks; they aren't quid pro quos. Rather, they are declarations of what already is for those who follow Jesus. Perhaps each sentence could just as easily begin with "congratulations."

Congratulations to those who are poor in spirit, because theirs is the kingdom of heaven.

Congratulations to those who mourn because they shall be comforted.

Congratulations to those who are meek because they shall inherit the earth.

Congratulations to those who ... and so on and so forth ... because God's favor is already upon them.

And the whole point is that God's favor is better than temporal happiness, contrary to the "pursue your own happiness no matter the cost" culture we live in. Happiness, by definition, is conditional, which means it's dependent on momentary circumstances—our happenings—and is therefore fleeting. But the blessings Jesus spoke of point to a fuller, more significant kind of human flourishing. Not in the material sense like those who seem to have it all, but in the faith-affirming, peace-abiding, future-securing sense our souls truly long for.

Once we belong to Him, we're ushered into that new reality where momentary suffering is eclipsed by God's immediate favor, His permanent presence, and the imperishable riches He's setting aside in heaven for those who choose to remain steadfast and continually invest in His kingdom.

Your Turn

8. Peter said that God had plans from "before the foundation of the world" for Jesus to suffer and die and be raised to life *for our sake*. What reassurance do you find in the idea that God has long-planned goals for hardship?

Prayer Focus

Praise God for the blessing of following Him on earth and for the beauty and reward that await you in heaven. Thank Him for His generosity and extravagant love freely offered to you through Jesus. Confess the futile things you're still investing in, and ask for His help to choose what He cares about instead.

Sample Prayer

Hear this, all peoples! Give ear, all inhabitants of the world, both low and high, rich and poor together! My mouth shall speak wisdom; the meditation of my heart shall be understanding. I will incline my ear to a proverb; I will solve my riddle to the music of the lyre. Why should I fear in times of trouble, when the iniquity of those who cheat me surrounds me, those who trust in their wealth and boast of the abundance of their riches? Truly no man can ransom another, or give to God the price of his life, for the ransom of their life is costly and can never suffice, that he should live on forever and never see the pit. For he sees that even the wise die; the fool and the stupid alike must perish and leave their wealth to others. Their graves are their homes forever, their dwelling places to all generations, though they called lands by their own names. Man in his pomp will not remain; he is like the beasts that perish. This is the path of those who have foolish confidence; yet after them people approve of their boasts. Like sheep they are appointed for Sheol; death shall be their shepherd, and the upright shall rule over them in the morning. Their form shall be consumed in Sheol, with no place to dwell. But God will ransom my soul from the power of Sheol, for he will receive me.

Psalm 49:1–15

ROAD TO BETHANY (DAY)

(The disciples struggle with the terrain and their pride.)

ANDREW: It's not that I'm humiliated—I am—it's that I'm so murderously angry they're doing this to Him.

PHILIP: I've done this plenty. Doesn't get any easier the next time.

(The Romans are rough but weary. Decanus senses a lull in his men and wants to get a laugh out of them. He takes Tamar's wrist and holds her arm up.)

DECANUS: Which one of you does this belong to?

(She wrenches free.)

ZEE: I never could have imagined a moment like this.

PETER: He said to submit. So ... we submit.

ZEE: The painful irony of some of His teaching.

DECANUS: You know what the holy men who perform the circumcisions say? "The pay is lousy, but we get to keep the tips."

(The disciples fume while the soldiers laugh. They approach a small sign pointing toward a Roman outpost.)

LEGIONNAIRE 2: Decanus, this sign is the mile marker.

DECANUS: In your entire lives, I bet you've never been so grateful for the enshrined Roman law.

LEGIONNAIRE 1: We know this has been an honor for all of you—

DECANUS: Stop here!

(Everyone stops but Jesus, who plods forward as if He didn't hear.)

DECANUS *(unnerved and suspicious)*: I said stop!

JESUS: Your destination is that outpost a mile ahead, yes?

LEGIONNAIRE 1: It is, but we're only permitted one mile.

JESUS: By coercion. There's no law against citizens assisting you the rest of the way of their own volition. Come, my friends.

DECANUS: But—

JESUS: If anyone says anything, say that we offered.

(He continues toward the outpost. The disciples follow without reservation, except—)

JUDAS: Rabbi? What are we doing? Why would we help Romans?

JESUS: Judas, where did we meet?

JUDAS: At the sermon on the Korazim plain.

JESUS: Good. Whenever you are troubled, think back on My message.

(Judas falls back in stunned silence. He watches as the group shuffles along. Finally, haltingly, Decanus sheepishly goes after Jesus in a strange display of embarrassment mixed with insistence.)

DECANUS *(removing his helmet from Jesus's head)*: Maybe, uh, let us take back the helmets ... so there's no confusion at the outpost.

JESUS: If you like.

(The other Romans, stammering, reclaim their helmets as well. They trade mystified looks amongst one another as they watch the disciples continue on.)

PHILIP *(muttering to Andrew)*: Hey—"if anyone forces you to go one mile ...

ANDREW: ... go with him two."

"Having purified
your souls by your
obedience to the truth for a sincere
brotherly love, love one another earnestly
from a pure heart, since you have been born
again, not of perishable seed but of imperishable,
through the living and abiding word of God; for
'All flesh is like grass
and all its glory like the flower of grass.
The grass withers,
and the flower falls,
but the word of the Lord remains forever.'
And this word is the good news that
was preached to you."

1 Peter 1:22–25

Lesson 6

Heartbreak is eclipsed by
LOVE

EXT. BETHANY—MARKET

(Peter, Matthew, Andrew, John, Big James, and Thomas shop the market.)

PETER: Thomas, let's check out the apothecary booths, huh? We're running low on soap.

THOMAS: That never seems to bother this group.

PETER: That's why I'm bringing you. I don't know anything about the finer things.
You know, Eden says I have no sense of smell or taste.

THOMAS: Is that true?

PETER: No. She says that I don't know what to call things, or I use the wrong words. I try
to compliment her cooking by saying something is sweet, but ... it wasn't meant to be sweet.
I just meant so good.

THOMAS *(handing a sample of a vendor's perfume to Peter)*: So what would you say this is?

PETER *(sniffing)*: I don't know ... some kind of flower?

THOMAS: Herbaceous. Close enough. *(Holding the dabber close to his nostril—)* Cedar
leaf and basil. Maybe a little lemon.

PETER: That's not close at all. You're just being nice.

THOMAS: I thought we were supposed to be looking for soap.

PETER: Thomas, how have you been feeling?

THOMAS: It's a feast time.

PETER: Well, you didn't answer me.

THOMAS: We're celebrating the Feast of Dedication. I'm supposed to feel grateful, I think?

PETER: Who cares what you're supposed to feel? Look, the Maccabees overthrew the Greeks so we could have full lives, not be wooden figures.

THOMAS: Then I feel horrible.

PETER: Thank you.

THOMAS: Thank you?

PETER: Yeah. For the truth. It's always the best place to start.

THOMAS: What I'm interested in is when it will end.

PETER: Is there any moment when you don't feel awful?

THOMAS: When we have some important work to do that takes my mind off things. If I can just think about the task at hand I'm okay, but apart from that ... in the stillness ... everything just ...

PETER: Aches.

THOMAS (*surprised*): You know?

PETER: I never met the person I lost.

THOMAS: Ramah told me about Eden's miscarriage. The women, they talk to each other about those kinds of things.

PETER: She tell you how badly I took it?

THOMAS: She didn't have to. I was on the boat, remember? You weren't subtle.

PETER: I don't know the meaning of the word. Do you remember what He said to me on the sea? That He allows trials because they prove the genuineness of our faith and strengthen us.

THOMAS: At the cost of someone's life?

PETER: I had the same thoughts in the depth of my pain, I assure you, and they only made things worse.

THOMAS: That doesn't make them wrong.

PETER: It's not wrong to question, but it does become wrong when you don't accept the answer.

THOMAS: I just don't understand *why* He didn't help Ramah. We've seen the miracles He does ... walking on water, multiplying food, powers that have not been seen manifested in the history of the earth. Why couldn't He have prevented her from being struck at all? Or even stopped time before her dying? Or even bring her back?

PETER: When I turn these things over in my mind, I go back to what God said through the prophet Isaiah: "'My thoughts are not your thoughts, neither are my ways your ways,' declares the Lord." You know, He can create a world where we have no free will and where nothing ever goes wrong, but that's clearly the future, it's not now.

THOMAS: Don't throw scraps of prophets around, Peter. I know all the same words. Were they any help to you?

(Arriving at the soap vendor, Thomas selects one block that he hands to Peter.)

THOMAS (CONT'D): Here. This one for the women.

PETER *(sniffing it)*: Cloves?

THOMAS: Nope. Lavender oil. And these two for the guys.

PETER *(sniffing again)*: Okay I've got this one ... wet moss.

THOMAS: Vetiver and basil.

PETER: Maybe I am a lost cause.

THOMAS: Absolutely.

Heart of the Matter

For most of us, following Jesus isn't always what it's cracked up to be. Sounds irreverent, but it's true because even when we're not trying to, we have preconceived notions about what God should do, where He should lead, and how He should intervene in our lives—including all the ways we think He should prevent our suffering.

The same thing was true for the disciples. Not only did Jesus require them to do surprisingly hard things, but the opposition to what they were doing continued to grow—all the way up to the moment when Jesus and (presumably) His followers were run outta town by a murderous mob (John 10:22–42). And then to top it off, they received word that their good friend Lazarus was dead (John 11:1–16).

For Bible Nerds (like us) Who Want to Know

The Gospel of John tells us more about the apostle Thomas than any other New Testament writer does. John regularly referred to him as "the Twin" (which is the Greek equivalent of the Hebrew and/or Aramaic name, "Thomas").

Nevertheless, instead of "the Twin," people today usually dub him as "Doubting Thomas" due to his refusal to believe in the resurrection of Jesus until he had substantial proof. Meaning, he wanted to see Jesus in the flesh with his own eyes:

"So the other disciples told [Thomas], 'We have seen the Lord.' But he said to them, 'Unless I see in his hands the mark of the nails, and place my finger into the mark of the nails, and place my hand into his side, I will never believe.'

Eight days later, his disciples were inside again, and Thomas was with them. Although the doors were locked, Jesus came and stood among them and said, 'Peace be with you.'

Then he said to Thomas, 'Put your finger here, and see my hands; and put out your hand, and place it in my side. Do not disbelieve, but believe.'

Thomas answered him, 'My Lord and my God!' Jesus said to him, 'Have you believed because you have seen me? Blessed are those who have not seen and yet have believed'" (John 20:25–29).

But the incident in John 11 shows a different side of Thomas. When Jesus told the group they were going to the already dead Lazarus, back in the dangerous Judean region from which they had just fled for their lives(!), Thomas spoke up: "Let us also go, that we may die with him" (John 11:16).

What can be credited as raw courage, was also tainted by pessimism because while Thomas was willing to choose death with Jesus (and Lazarus), his statement suggested that he wasn't reassured by Jesus's own words (see vv. 9–10). And he certainly wasn't yet understanding that Jesus alone would sacrificially die for him and everyone else.

Sometime after, Thomas asked the clarifying question about the way of salvation (14:5), to which Jesus responded, "I am the way, and the truth, and the life. No one comes to the Father except through me" (14:6).

So, we can be grateful for Thomas's example of courage in his willingness to follow Jesus unto death, but also in his willingness to honestly express doubt and ask hard questions. As a result, his faith was strengthened, as is ours.

It wasn't how they assumed people would respond to the Messiah, or the reward they expected to receive for following Him, or the way they hoped Jesus would care for one of His closest friends. After all, He had healed so many others. But upon hearing Lazarus was near death, "he stayed two days longer in the place where he was" (John 11:6).

Truth be told, little of what the disciples experienced lined up with their preconceived notions. Not only were their circumstances brutal, so was the fact that Jesus didn't prevent or respond or intervene in ways that would've spared them much heartache.

And now we've arrived at the heart of the matter.

Your Turn

1. In spite of following Jesus, the twelve apostles still faced loss and heartbreak. And like them, sometimes our circumstances profoundly disappoint us regarding the ways Jesus is working (or seemingly *not* working) in our lives.

What are some of your preconceived notions about Jesus and what following Him should be like? What are some of your profound disappointments?

Land of the Living

"As for man, his days are like grass; he flourishes like a flower of the field; for the wind passes over it, and it is gone, and its place knows it no more."

Psalm 103:15–16

As much as we like to think of ourselves as strong, capable, and important, according to Scripture, humanity is actually frail, desperate, and easily forgotten. We're like flowers that fall, grass that withers, mist that vanishes. We are dust, and "to dust [we] shall return" (Gen. 3:19). Which means any and all human achievement is temporary and, as Peter said, cannot accomplish what the eternal word of God can accomplish.

What it *has* accomplished and *will* accomplish.

But that doesn't stop us from trying. Oh, how we try. We strive and strain and reach and run toward the things we want ... but also away from suffering. Indeed, we usually see suffering as being the opposite of good. We try to avoid difficult circumstances, and we fear pain, all the while knowing it's impossible to go through life without eventually experiencing all of it.

Lest we despair over our fleeting earthly existence and the weakness and heartache therein, Peter (an experienced sufferer) reminds us that God has intervened already, and that through Jesus's life, death, and resurrection we are born again, "not of perishable seed but of imperishable" (1 Pet. 1:23). In other words, God has made us spiritually new and promised us an eternal home, one where (a) our names will not only be remembered, they'll be memorialized, and (b) pain, weakness, hardship, and heartbreak will be no more.

But we're not there yet. So, in the meantime, we hold fast to hope and soldier on, with new hearts that are being filled with all the fullness of God.

Your Turn

2. In what way(s) have you experienced your own weakness and frailty?

3. If life is fleeting, so is any pain and heartbreak that comes your way. How does that change the way you view suffering?

"The one who conquers will be clothed thus in white garments, and I will never blot his name out of the book of life. I will confess his name before my Father and before his angels."
Revelation 3:5

God's word is eternally effective; it abides.

Abide:
to continue without fading.

4. What does it mean that God's word "abides"? In what ways are you encouraged to know that "you have been born again, not of perishable seed but of imperishable, through the living and *abiding* word of God" (1 Pet. 1:23)?

"Heaven and earth will pass away, but my words will not pass away."
Matthew 24:35

New Life, New Love

"For this reason I bow my knees before the Father, from

whom every family in heaven and on earth is named,

that according to the riches of his glory he may grant

you to be strengthened with power through his Spirit in

your inner being, so that Christ may dwell in your hearts

through faith—that you, being rooted and grounded in

love, may have strength to comprehend with all the saints

what is the breadth and length and height and depth,

and to know the love of Christ that surpasses knowledge,

that you may be filled with all the fullness of God."

Ephesians 3:14–19

When we're spiritually reborn, Christ takes up residency in our hearts and He becomes our source of strength and love, no matter the circumstance. And that's the key to living a godly, obedient life on this otherwise withering, broken planet:

Love.

Indeed, love is the natural and right response of God's children to His loving intervention through Christ (i.e., Jesus and "the good news that was preached to you"). But it isn't just our salvation that motivates and empowers us to love each other. Rather, the command to "love one another earnestly" is grounded in the eternality of our salvation. Because Christians have been born into eternal life, we must live in sincere brotherly love for one another in an eternal community of faith, one that reflects (a) we are God's children and God *is* love and (b) we are heaven-bound where we'll live together in the place He's preparing for us.

"Love one another earnestly from a pure heart, since you have been born again, not of perishable seed but of imperishable …"

"Beloved, let us love one another, for love is from God, and whoever loves has been born of God and knows God. Anyone who does not love does not know God, because God is love. In this the love of God was made manifest among us, that God sent his only Son into the world, so that we might live through him. In this is love, not that we have loved God but that he loved us and sent his Son to be the propitiation for our sins. Beloved, if God so loved us, we also ought to love one another. No one has ever seen God; if we love one another, God abides in us and his love is perfected in us."
1 John 4:7–12

"Let not your hearts be troubled. Believe in God; believe also in me. In my Father's house are many rooms. If it were not so, would I have told you that I go to prepare a place for you? And if I go and prepare a place for you, I will come again and will take you to myself, that where I am you may be also."
John 14:1–3

Keeping our eyes fixed on that forever home and family eases the heartbreak we experience while waiting for eternity to commence—because we know our time here is short, so any and all suffering is temporary and will be eclipsed by the joy that is to come. We know that, in time, God is going to heal what's broken and restore His creation. And we know that Christ's love, which dwells in our hearts through faith, is the very thing that will draw other heartbroken people to Him.

Christ's love is the balm for our grieving souls.

Your Turn

5. We typically think of love as a feeling that overcomes us and determines our actions. But 1 John 4:7–12 describes love as a decision. What connections do you see between love and obedience? How is loving obedience different from feelings that ebb and flow?

6. In what ways does having an eternal community of faith help to ease your present heartbreak?

7. How will you obey the command to "love one another earnestly from a pure heart" today?

Following Orders

"We love because he first loved us. If anyone says, 'I love God,' and hates
his brother, he is a liar; for he who does not love his brother whom he has
seen cannot love God whom he has not seen. And this commandment
we have from him: whoever loves God must also love his brother.
Everyone who believes that Jesus is the Christ has been born of God,
and everyone who loves the Father loves whoever has been born of him.
By this we know that we love the children of God, when we love God
and obey his commandments. For this is the love of God, that we keep
his commandments. And his commandments are not burdensome."

1 John 4:19–5:3

Loving one another is not a suggestion; it's an order. But we follow orders because we love the One who loved us first (Rom. 5:8). The One who guards and protects us (John 10:11–18). The One who keeps and leads us (Heb. 13:20–21). We obey His command to love because we're so fully and completely loved by Him already (Rom. 8:32). And when we share His love, we're participating in spreading the good news of the gospel because there's simply no better way to meet the needs of the moment we're living in.

The world is indeed full of so much heartbreak, from which the followers of Jesus are not always protected. But the balm of Christ's presence, power, and love is healing and ultimately eclipses the pain inflicted upon us by the broken world we live in.

The broken world we live in just for now.

Your Turn

8. How is God's love eclipsing your heartbreak?

Prayer Focus

Meditate on God's love for you in Christ Jesus. Thank Him for His loving intervention, and that He continues to pursue your heart. Tell Him about your heartbreak and ask for more of His wisdom and strength to endure. Pray for healing. Pray for more faith and the ability to hope in what is eternal and waiting for you, just around the bend.

Sample Prayer

I love the LORD, because he has heard my voice and my pleas for mercy. Because he inclined his ear to me, therefore I will call on him as long as I live. The snares of death encompassed me; the pangs of Sheol laid hold on me; I suffered distress and anguish. Then I called on the name of the LORD: "O LORD, I pray, deliver my soul!" Gracious is the LORD, and righteous; our God is merciful. The LORD preserves the simple; when I was brought low, he saved me. Return, O my soul, to your rest; for the LORD has dealt bountifully with you. For you have delivered my soul from death, my eyes from tears, my feet from stumbling; I will walk before the LORD in the land of the living. I believed, even when I spoke: "I am greatly afflicted"; I said in my alarm, "All mankind are liars." What shall I render to the LORD for all his benefits to me? I will lift up the cup of salvation and call on the name of the LORD, I will pay my vows to the LORD in the presence of all his people. Precious in the sight of the LORD is the death of his saints. O LORD, I am your servant; I am your servant, the son of your maidservant. You have loosed my bonds. I will offer to you the sacrifice of thanksgiving and call on the name of the LORD. I will pay my vows to the LORD in the presence of all his people, in the courts of the house of the LORD, in your midst, O Jerusalem. Praise the LORD!

Psalm 116

EXT. TEMPLE COURTS (GOLDEN HOUR)

(Passing by the Livestock Exchange, Jesus notices a shepherd selling his sheep to the Pharisee Livestock Inspectors. He pets the wool of one of them fondly. He addresses His followers—)

JESUS: Listen carefully ... he who does not enter the sheepfold by the door but climbs in by another way, that man is a thief and a robber. But he who enters by the door is the shepherd of the sheep. The sheep hear his voice, and he calls his own sheep by name and leads them out. When he has brought out all his own, he goes before them, and the sheep follow him, for they know his voice.

(The Livestock Pharisees notice Jesus is here. They grab each other's attention.)

In episode 6, Jesus and His followers recite portions of the Hallel Psalms as part of their celebration of the ancient Jewish holiday. The word *hallel* means "praise," and Psalms 113–118 are commonly called the Hallel Psalms, or sometimes more simply, the Hallel.

JESUS (CONT'D): They won't follow a stranger, but they will flee from him, for they do not know the voice of strangers.

NATHANAEL (as confused as everyone else): I'm uh … not sure I follow.

PETER: This … figure of speech you're using … could you say it more plainly?

ANDREW: We want to understand.

(The Pharisees are now within earshot, scrutinizing everything.)

JESUS: This is important … I am the door of the sheep. All who came before Me are thieves and robbers, but the sheep did not listen to them.

(Pharisees now whispering to one another.)

JESUS (CONT'D): I am the door. If anyone enters by Me, he will be saved and will go in and out and find pasture. The thief comes only to steal and kill and destroy.

(The disciples listen closely, but Judas is paying more attention to the growing group of Pharisees.)

JESUS (CONT'D): I came that they may have life and have it abundantly. I am the good shepherd. The good shepherd lays down his life for His sheep. He who is a hired hand and not a shepherd, who does not own the sheep, sees the wolf coming and leaves the sheep and flees, and the wolf snatches them and scatters them. He flees because he is a hired hand and cares nothing for the sheep. I am the good shepherd. I know My own and My own know Me, just as the Father knows Me and I know the Father; and I lay down My life for the sheep.

OZEM: He fits the description of a man we're looking for. Do you know who he is?

PHARISEE 1: Not yet, I was waiting for you.

(A couple of the disciples are noticing they suddenly have company.)

JESUS: And I have other sheep that are not of this fold. I must bring them also, and they will listen to My voice.

OZEM (loud and interrupting): "Other sheep not of this fold" … Are you referring to Gentiles?

JESUS: So there will be one flock, one shepherd. For this reason the Father loves Me, because I lay down My life that I may take it up again.

GEDERA: That's not real. There is no resurrection.

ZEBEDIAH: At least not one that any mortal man could have authority to enact for himself, once perished.

JUDAS *(in a hushed tone to Peter—)*: We need to do something!

PETER: Just pay attention, Judas.

OZEM: Someone has to go get Shammai immediately!

ZEBEDIAH: He's gone for the holiday.

JUDAS *(now to Matthew—)*: How can we pay attention with these men talking and insulting Him?

MATTHEW: Jesus never specified what to pay attention to.

JESUS *(wrapping up and looking directly at the Pharisees)*: No one takes it from Me, but I lay it down of My own accord. I have authority to lay it down, and I have authority to take it up again. This charge I have received from My Father.

"So put away all malice and all deceit and hypocrisy and envy and all slander. Like newborn infants, long for the pure spiritual milk, that by it you may grow up into salvation—if indeed you have tasted that the Lord is good."

1 Peter 2:1–3

Lesson 7

Contamination is eclipsed by
DEDICATION

MOUNTAINS OF LA SAINTE BAUME—CAVE—SUPER: AD 60

(Matthew and Magdalene make their way deep into a cave. The interior is illuminated by candles. Clearly she's been living here for some time.)

MAGDALENE: Careful, it's very dark. Watch where you step ... I can't believe you came all this way, Matthew, with the danger and at your age!

MATTHEW *(chuckling)*: Our age. It was important. *(pulling a huge leather folio of parchment out of his bag, bound with string)* Mary, I finished it.

MAGDALENE *(astonished)*: The book?

MATTHEW: I couldn't risk sending it by courier. I wanted you to be the first one to read it, please. And I want to hear your thoughts. I had to be here for it.

MAGDALENE *(tears filling her eyes, she carefully accepts the enormous folio as the priceless artifact it is)*: I can't believe it. You worked so hard. And for so long. This will be a treasure for all time.

MATTHEW: I'm here to see about that. It will outlive us. We know that much.

MAGDALENE: I know I'm right.

MATTHEW: Before we say anything further, I'm afraid I have some bad news.

MAGDALENE: I've gotten used to that.

MATTHEW: This I could have sent word of, but I thought since I was coming here to see you, I would tell you in person.

(He struggles. She puts him out of his misery.)

MAGDALENE: Who is it?

MATTHEW *(swallowing hard)*: Little James.

(Magdalene closes her eyes, lets out air and emotion. She finds her voice to ask for details.)

MAGDALENE: How did it happen? Where?

MATTHEW: Mary, if you don't—

MAGDALENE *(firm)*: No, I want to know, I can handle it. Tell me.

MATTHEW: Lower Egypt. King Hircanus had him run through with a spear.

(An involuntary cry escapes Magdalene. Even after all the news of all the deaths, it still hits her hard every time.)

MAGDALENE: What about Onya and the girls?

MATTHEW: Mercifully, they were not there to see it.

MAGDALENE: Thanks be to God.

MATTHEW: Zee's men are moving them to stay with Nympha and her husband at Colossae. Paul has been sending letters to the church there.

MAGDALENE: They should be safe there. I'll send a letter to Onya.

MATTHEW: What will you say to her?

MAGDALENE *(after a beat)*: That he's not suffering anymore. He was in pain his entire life and he so rarely complained.

(This aspect had not occurred to Matthew. He's moved. Mary wipes her tears and returns her attention to the task at hand—)

MAGDALENE (CONT'D): I'm going to stay up all night and read your manuscript. I want to relive it all. Even the hard parts.

(Something is off with Matthew, and Magdalene notices.)

MAGDALENE (CONT'D): Is something wrong? That is why you came, isn't it?

MATTHEW: It is. It's just, something I noticed …

(His gaze shifts to her desk in the corner, strewn about with fragments of parchment. She follows his gaze.)

MAGDALENE: My desk? I write letters there.

MATTHEW: I apologize—I don't mean to pry … I just noticed as I passed by … those scraps don't look like letters.

MAGDALENE: You read them?

MATTHEW: No! No, I would never. The pieces sitting there struck me as … odd?

MAGDALENE: Matthew, let me read your volume. Don't busy yourself with my scribblings.

MATTHEW: I am sure they're more substantial than scribblings.

MAGDALENE: Why are we talking about this?

MATTHEW: Parchment is expensive. You live in a cave on a mountainside far from merchants or civilization. No one in your position, or mine, wastes paper.

MAGDALENE: It's true. I'm not wasteful.

MATTHEW: Mary, I value your thoughts and I am eager to hear them all. Will you allow me? *(He's shifts.)* It's fine. You know I'm here for you. Now and always.

MAGDALENE *(pained)*: I've been having dreams lately. About some of the darker times. In my life and His … and others among us. I wanted to write them down so I don't forget, trying to assemble them into … something. I don't know. Just for me, no one else.

MATTHEW: I understand. I'm sorry to have pried. I would only want you to share if you felt comfortable sharing.

MAGDALENE *(following a long hard look at Matthew, she turns her gaze back to the desk and softens)*: Perhaps I can share it with you, my oldest friend.

Contaminants

In first-century Jewish culture, there was a ton of focus on things that contaminate. Mind you, it wasn't because the people were germophobes. Rather than notions of personal hygiene for the protection of physical health, the people were concerned about "purity" because it symbolized spiritual health. To that end, the Israelite priests were "to distinguish between the holy and the common, and between the unclean and the clean," in order "to teach the people of Israel all the statutes that the LORD [had] spoken to them by Moses" (Lev. 10:10–11).

To that end, purity laws were far reaching and had implications for what food could be consumed (Lev. 11), how to manage childbirth (Lev. 12), how to interact with sick people (Lev. 13–14), how to treat bodily discharges (Lev. 15), and how to handle human corpses (Num. 19). Of course, some forms of impurity were unavoidable in day-to-day life and weren't considered sinful in and of themselves (for example, when people died, their corpses *had* to be handled in order to bury them). But the recognition of those things as forms of impurity still demanded symbolic purification, which brought to the forefront the people's awareness of their need for a Savior (our permanent spiritual purification).

For Bible Nerds (like us) Who Want to Know

In the symbolism of ritual purity practices, of the various forms of contamination, the ultimate impurity was death. In episode 7, when Jesus and the group of His followers hear about Lazarus's death, Jesus announces that they will go back to Judea where their lives had just been threatened. As the group is en route, John and Thomas discuss death, and John asks about Thomas's earlier remark, "Let us also go, that we may die with him" (John 11:16). John tries to encourage Thomas to recognize that death is not an honorable goal in life. But Thomas tries to help John recognize that death is a fact of life: "We have been forced to accept that death is a part of life."

And certainly Thomas is correct: death is a fact of life.

But that's not the final word on the topic. Elsewhere in the group, Mary Magdalene and Little James ponder Psalm 13 (see page 54). Contemplating the biblical phrase "lest I sleep the sleep of death," Little James notes that sometimes the terms "sleep" and "death" are used interchangeably. Then Mary notes that perhaps it's possible to be "awakened" from death, which is why she said, "We'll sit shiva, or we won't," because she understands that Jesus is powerful enough to cleanse a person from the ultimate impurity symbol: death.

Indeed, that's precisely what happens. Jesus "awakens" Lazarus from the "sleep" of death. Of course, we know from Scripture that not long after, Jesus Himself rose from the dead, proving once and for all that He is our permanent spiritual purification.

Fast-forward to what Peter said about purity in terms of obedience and love: "Having purified your souls by your obedience to the truth for a sincere brotherly love, love one another earnestly from a pure heart" (1 Pet. 1:22). After which, he provided a short list of things that contaminate that love: "So put away all malice and all deceit and hypocrisy and envy and all slander" (2:1). Such things derail the love believers share within the community of faith, making them worse than the actual physical diseases people tried to avoid because these evils threaten what new life in Jesus is supposed to be.

It's supposed to be good.

Your Turn

1. Early followers of Christ understood the importance of belonging to a loving community and "putting away" contaminants that threatened that community. Which of Peter's examples (malice, deceit, hypocrisy, envy, slander) do you find most difficult to put away? What are some others you struggle with that Peter didn't specifically mention here?

Disinfecting Light

"But we have renounced disgraceful, underhanded ways. We refuse to practice cunning or to tamper with God's word, but by the open statement of the truth we would commend ourselves to everyone's conscience in the sight of God."

2 Corinthians 4:2

Commend: to entrust someone or something to. In other words, "we entrust ourselves to you in the sight of God, our actions transparent and in full view."

Jesus came to save us from the contamination of sin; that's 100 percent true. But He also came to save us for new life in Him that offers a restored relationship with God the Father and an ongoing community within His family of believers. Of course, without Jesus, sin stands between us and God—an insurmountable blockade that casts a long shadow of darkness and death. To that end, it keeps us isolated from our loving Father, as well as other believers, because (among sin's other contaminations in our lives) we work hard to hide the things we don't want anyone to see.

But God.

"But God demonstrates his own love for us in this: While we were still sinners, Christ died for us" (Rom. 5:8 NIV).

As followers of Jesus and because of God's love, we step into "the light of the gospel of the glory of Christ, who is the image of God" (2 Cor. 4:4). And that light disinfects because the things that once contaminated our hearts along with our relationships are (a) illuminated by the Holy Spirit through conviction of sin (John 16:7–11), (b) forgiven when we confess (1 John 1:9–10), (c) resisted with the strength and self-control He provides (2 Tim. 1:7), and (d) right-sized with accountability and support from our brothers and sisters in the faith (Gal. 6:1–2).

We "commend ourselves to everyone's conscience in the sight of God" because we've been forgiven and *made* pure by Jesus. To that end, there's nothing left to hide. We can be transparent and honest and authentic with others about our victories as well as our ongoing struggles because we've been forgiven and accepted by God into His community.

And because of that, it's time to grow up.

Your Turn

2. How do you feel about God's disinfecting—i.e., sin-exposing—light?

3. Why is it important for us to be in community with other believers?

4. What keeps you from entrusting yourself to the Jesus followers around you? What needs to change in order for you to lean into those relationships more?

For Bible Nerds (like us) Who Want to Know

The Gospel of John records some of Jesus's emotion in the story of Lazarus's raising. He was "deeply moved in his spirit and greatly troubled" (11:33); "Jesus wept" (v. 35); He was "deeply moved again" (v. 38); and in commanding the dead man to rise, He "cried out with a loud voice" (v. 43).

Jesus wasn't merely grieving over His friend's death or that Lazarus's friends and relatives were grieving too. To be sure, Jesus was expressing the emotion of sadness here, but there's more. The "deeply moved" term used twice in the story is best understood as Jesus being "outraged"; He was not merely sad, but angry with what was happening.

Some scholars have suggested Jesus was angry at sickness itself, along with sin and death in the human experience, and how those things cause so much sorrow. Others have suggested Jesus was angry that the expressions of grief had risen to the point of unbelief—that the people were grieving as if there was no hope of resurrection (see 1 Thess. 4:13), that the people's grief was betraying a lack of faith.

Perhaps it was both. Perhaps Jesus was outraged over the fact that sin and sickness have led humanity to be captive to death and He was angry at the specific sin of disbelief in God's power to raise the dead.

Taste and See

"Taste and see that the LORD is good; blessed

is the one who takes refuge in him."

Psalm 34:8 (NIV)

Believing God and what He says about sin means we renounce what He deems disgraceful and underhanded. It also means we embrace our lives in Christ along with the things He says are good—things like authenticity within our God-given communities and the "fruit" He's producing inside our hearts.

To that end, Peter encouraged his readers to grow in faith by becoming like babies. Of course, he wasn't intending for Christians to be child*ish* but instead to be child*like*. Or, more precisely, to be like children who want to grow. "Like newborn infants, long for the pure spiritual milk, that by it you may grow up into salvation" (1 Pet. 2:2). And the life-giving, life-sustaining Word of God is the source of that pure spiritual milk. Indeed, reading, hearing, and studying the Bible enable our growth in the faith.

Mind you, spiritual growth refers to direction, not perfection. Because even when we agree with God about our sin, it remains a potential struggle on this side of eternity. As Paul said:

For I have the desire to do what is right, but not the ability to carry it out.

For I do not do the good I want, but the evil I do not want is what I keep on doing. Now if I do what I do not want, it is no longer I who do it, but sin that dwells within me.

So I find it to be a law that when I want to do right, evil lies close at hand. For I delight in the law of God, in my inner being, but I see in my members another law waging war against the law of my mind and making me captive to the law of sin that dwells in my members. Wretched man that I am! Who will deliver me from this body of death? Thanks be to God through Jesus Christ our Lord! (Rom. 7:18–25)

Like Peter (and Paul, who wrote the NT book of Romans), we must repeatedly choose to put contaminants away. We must remain honest with ourselves and those we trust that we're still prone to sin. And we must embrace spiritual goodness and growth because of the Lord's goodness to us. In fact, the faithful apostle instructed his readers to *long* for growth since "you have tasted that the Lord is good" (1 Pet. 2:3).

Experiencing goodness from the Lord—His grace, forgiveness, healing power, and unwavering love (just to name a few)—encourages us to look to His Word in order *to hear more from Him*. To dedicate time in prayer in order *to be led more by Him*. To lean into our relationship with Him as well as those He's placed in our lives in order *to be more obedient to Him*. And as a result of that obedience, we taste and see His goodness again and again in our lives.

And who doesn't want *more* of what's good?

For Bible Nerds (like us) Who Want to Know

Peter further described brotherly love (which includes sisterly love ☺) in 1 Peter 3:8–12, where he quoted Psalm 34:12–16 about seeing good days as a result of obedient living:

"Finally, all of you, have unity of mind, sympathy, brotherly love, a tender heart, and a humble mind. Do not repay evil for evil or reviling for reviling, but on the contrary, bless, for to this you were called, that you may obtain a blessing. For 'whoever desires to love life and see good days, let him keep his tongue from evil and his lips from speaking deceit; let him turn away from evil and do good; let him seek peace and pursue it. For the eyes of the Lord are on the righteous, and his ears are open to their prayer. But the face of the Lord is against those who do evil.'"

Your Turn

5. What good things have you experienced from the Lord?

6. Paul's response to his sin in Romans 7:24–25 was twofold:

a. He recognized his propensity for sin: "Wretched man that I am! Who will deliver me from this body of death?"

b. He praised God for saving him from sin: "Thanks be to God through Jesus Christ our Lord!"

In what ways do those statements encourage you to remain dedicated to growing in faith and in your relationship with Jesus?

For Bible Nerds (like us) Who Want to Know

The familiar story of Lazarus recorded in chapter 11 of the Gospel of John mentions that each of his sisters—Martha and Mary (a popular name in that day!)—said to Jesus, "Lord, if you had been here, my brother would not have died" (vv. 21, 32).

It seems that, while both of them had faith that Jesus could heal the sick, neither of them were ready for a raising from the dead. To be sure, Martha believed in a future, end-times resurrection. When Jesus said, "Your brother will rise again," she professed, "I know that he will rise again in the resurrection on the last day" (vv. 23–24).

Jesus confirmed her expression of faith: "I am the resurrection and the life. Whoever believes in me, though he die, yet shall he live, and everyone who lives and believes in me shall never die" (vv. 25–26).

But He was intending to give an advanced taste of that resurrection power by raising Lazarus from the dead that very day! Which means their suffering was eclipsed by the good thing—the far better thing—God was doing in and through it.

7. What changes can you make today in order to grow more, in order to *experience more*, of God's goodness?

Dedication

> "I appeal to you therefore, brothers, by the mercies of God, to present
> your bodies as a living sacrifice, holy and acceptable to God, which
> is your spiritual worship. Do not be conformed to this world, but be
> transformed by the renewal of your mind, that by testing you may discern
> what is the will of God, what is good and acceptable and perfect."
>
> Romans 12:1–2

This world is full of brokenness, hardship, trials, pain, and even death. But it's also full of God's goodness because His presence, power, and plans for each one of us remain firmly in place. He works in and through our suffering to cleanse us of contaminants and grow our faith, along with our capacity to endure trials. He teaches our hearts to hope in heaven and to praise Him while we wait for it to commence. He is wholly dedicated to caring for those of us who follow Jesus—which is why we should wholly dedicate ourselves right back to Him. Indeed, all the things we do, all the words we say, and every moment we spend this side of heaven should be done "in the name of the Lord Jesus, giving thanks to God the Father through him" (Col. 3:17).

Why?

Because He's good! And because we want more of His goodness. And because we believe Him when He tells us that dedicated obedience to Him is the way we'll experience more of that goodness. And because through trials and, yes, suffering, we've come to understand that His will and ways are good, acceptable, and perfect.

Just like He said.

"I have said these things to you, that in me you may have peace. In the world you will have tribulation. But take heart; I have overcome the world" (John 16:33).

Your Turn

8. In what ways have sin or suffering in your life been eclipsed by obedience to the Lord and by His goodness that flows through it?

Prayer Focus

Praise Jesus for being your permanent spiritual purification. Thank Him for your community of believers, and for the opportunity to love others the way God has loved you. Ask for courage and strength to obey more and more, and for opportunities to taste and see that obedience is worth the sacrifice it requires.

Sample Prayer

O LORD, I call upon you; hasten to me! Give ear to my voice when I call to you! Let my prayer be counted as incense before you, and the lifting up of my hands as the evening sacrifice! Set a guard, O LORD, over my mouth; keep watch over the door of my lips! Do not let my heart incline to any evil, to busy myself with wicked deeds in company with men who work iniquity, and let me not eat of their delicacies! Let a righteous man strike me—it is a kindness; let him rebuke me—it is oil for my head; let my head not refuse it. Yet my prayer is continually against their evil deeds. When their judges are thrown over the cliff, then they shall hear my words, for they are pleasant. As when one plows and breaks up the earth, so shall our bones be scattered at the mouth of Sheol. But my eyes are toward you, O GOD, my Lord; in you I seek refuge; leave me not defenseless! Keep me from the trap that they have laid for me and from the snares of evildoers! Let the wicked fall into their own nets, while I pass by safely.

Psalm 141

INT. MOUNTAINS OF LA SAINTE BAUME—CAVE (NIGHT)

(Back to AD 60, elderly Magdalene somewhat nervously gathers up the fragments of her notes on the desk. Matthew settles into a chair nearby. As she arranges the notes—)

MAGDALENE: The more I read the songs of David, the more I felt I needed to write one of my own. Please just know that whatever this is going to be is not finished.

MATTHEW: You so rarely let people into your mind. But the times you did, I was always grateful.

(She acknowledges this politely, but doesn't say anything. The wind outside the caves moans and haunts. Finally, she clears her throat.)

MAGDALENE: Darkness is not the absence of light. That would be too simple. It's more uncontrollable and sinister. Not a place but a void. I was there once. More than once. And although I couldn't see or hear You, You were there, waiting.

(We see a series of present-day scenes as word of Jesus's final miracle spreads. Elderly Mary's psalm is continually heard over all of it.)

HOME OF LAZARUS (NIGHT)

(Lazarus holds the sodden burial linens in his hands and ponders in the candlelight.)

MAGDALENE: Because the darkness is not dark to You. At least, not always.

HOME OF ARNÁN (NIGHT)

(Arnán rushes up the stairs to Yussif's bedroom, rustling him awake.)

MAGDALENE: You wept, not because Your friend was dead, but because You soon would be.

HOME OF SHMUEL (NIGHT)

(Shmuel wakes up to door knocking. And just like season 3, he opens his door to reveal a young Pharisee.)

MAGDALENE: And because we couldn't understand it, or didn't want to, or both.

HOME OF SHAMMAI (NIGHT)
(Sadducee pounds on the door of a huge house until it opens to reveal Shammai in a nightgown with a candle. His look of inconvenience vanishes the moment he takes in the countenance of the Sadducee.)

MAGDALENE: The coming darkness was too deep for us to grasp, but then so is the light. One had to come before the other.

HOME OF LAZARUS—OFFICE
(Mary of Bethany [who we'll call MARY B] enters Lazarus's office with a golden key, unlocks the safe, and takes three hundred denarii.)

MAGDALENE: It was always that way with You. It still is. Tears fell from Your eyes, and then ours, before every light in the world went out and time itself wanted to die with You.

HOME OF LAZARUS—GUEST ROOMS
(In one of the rooms, Peter finishes cleaning and redressing Big James's head wound, then helps him carefully get into bed.)

MAGDALENE: I go back to that place sometimes. Or rather, it comes back to me, uninvited ...

(Across the room Little James struggles to find a comfortable position. Zee uses a candle snuffer to put out each of the lights in the room. From the exterior we see another window go dark.)

MAGDALENE: ... the night that was eternal, until it wasn't. Bitter, and then sweet, but somehow the bitter remained in the sweet and has never gone away.

(Lying on his mat, Thomas gazes at the sundial that he gave Ramah, wanting to smash it into a thousand pieces.)

MAGDALENE: You told us it would be like that. Not with words, but with how You lived, the Man of Sorrows, acquainted with grief.

(Thomas tucks the sundial into a cotton pouch next to his mat, which John witnesses, then blows out the candle and from the exterior we see another of the windows go dark.)

MAGDALENE: That grief wasn't what we wanted to see, so we tried to look away, and in so doing fulfilled Your very essence: "one from whom people hide their faces."

HOME OF LAZARUS—WOMEN'S QUARTERS
(Tamar beds down in the upstairs women's room. Magdalene goes to the window and snuffs out a candle, the final light of the house. But something outside on the ground below catches her eye. It's Jesus, taking in the sight of the broken pitcher that Thomas shattered at the well.)

MAGDALENE: But soon we couldn't hide from it any more than we could stop the sun from setting. Or rising.

HOME OF LAZARUS—BEDROOM

(Jesus puts two of the broken shards together, like jigsaw puzzle pieces, but they are not magically joined in a miracle. They stay in two separate pieces. He gently fingers the razor-sharp edge of the shard, thinking of the days ahead.)

MAGDALENE: I remember You wishing there could be another way, and looking back I do too.

TOMB OF LAZARUS (NIGHT)
(Slow push into the black void of Lazarus's empty tomb—)

MAGDALENE: I still don't know why it has to be this way ... the bitter, often mingled with the sweet. Maybe I never will. At least not this side of—

(When the void of the tomb fully envelops the frame, everything cuts to black and silence, like a power outage. There is a long, uncomfortable mute in the black. Finally—)
END CREDITS

"As you
come to him, a living
stone rejected by men but in the
sight of God chosen and precious, you
yourselves like living stones are being built up
as a spiritual house, to be a holy priesthood, to offer
spiritual sacrifices acceptable to God through Jesus
Christ. For it stands in Scripture: 'Behold, I am laying in Zion
a stone, a cornerstone chosen and precious, and whoever
believes in him will not be put to shame.' So the honor is
for you who believe, but for those who do not believe,
'The stone that the builders rejected has become the
cornerstone,' and 'A stone of stumbling, and a rock
of offense.' They stumble because they disobey
the word, as they were destined to do."

1 Peter 2:4-8

Lesson 8

Resistance is eclipsed by
RECEIVING

BETHANY—APOTHECARY

(A perfumer shows Mary B an array of essential oils.)

PERFUMER: This one is called "Cove." Three parts myrrh, two parts cassia, lovely for burning to purify a house. Ten denarii.

(Mary B politely smells the vial and shakes her head.)

PERFUMER (CONT'D): And this one is "Cleopatra." Four parts cypress, one part myrtle, in rose oil. Very good for skin and hair. Fifteen denarii, top shelf.

MARY B: Hmm. Not top shelf enough.

PERFUMER: Excuse me?

MARY B: I want to see your oils that aren't for sale. I know you have them; I've been to dinner with many wealthy people.

PERFUMER: I only bring those out for my most loyal and liquid customers.

(Mary B plops a velvet purse of coins onto the table. Perfumer is impressed but does her best to hide it. She looks inside the bag. Finally—)

In the Old Testament era, only the Israelite priests could approach God directly as they offered sacrifices in worship on behalf of the people. But now, due to Jesus's ultimate sacrifice on our behalf, He makes all of God's people into a "holy priesthood" able to approach God directly. As Peter states, our spiritual sacrifices are "acceptable to God through Jesus Christ."

Indeed, all believers get to not only look to Jesus, we get to come to Jesus. And those longing to grow in their faith by "feasting on" God's Word can! There is no need for a go-between.

PERFUMER (CONT'D): Wait here.

(*Perfumer disappears through a curtain for a moment, and we hear the sound of a safe opening and closing. She then brings out something bundled in silk.*)

PERFUMER (CONT'D): Derived from a rare flowering honeysuckle varietal high in the Nepal mountains, used to anoint kings in China and India, protected in a premium alabaster vessel for temperature control ... pure spikenard.

(*Perfumer reveals the alabaster jar. She pulls on a velvet glove, carefully uncorks the jar, and reverently dips in a sample stick. She holds up the sampling stick to Mary B's nose with her gloved hand beneath it to keep any oil from dripping. Truly impressed and a little overwhelmed by the aroma, Mary B's eyebrows go up.*)

PERFUMER (CONT'D): How many ounces would you like?

MARY B: The whole jar.

PERFUMER (*laughing*): Oh my, you are charming, dear. But truly, what do you think? One and a half ounces?

MARY B (*plopping down two more purses of coins onto the table*): I said the whole jar.

PERFUMER (*shocked and flummoxed*): I ... it's not possible ... this jar would cost more than half a year's wages, and I need the supply to satisfy my wealthiest clientele ... And it would take me several months to obtain another jar, it's—

MARY B (*adding the final purse of coins*): You need to listen. This is for the most important king the world has ever known. Three hundred denarii. A full year's wages.

(*Perfumer is agape. Mary B simply takes the jar and wraps it up in the silk.*)

MARY B (CONT'D): You can take the rest of the year off.

(*Mary B walks out with the jar, leaving Perfumer speechless.*)

No Shame

As this Bible study and our own life stories have revealed, following Jesus doesn't lead to earthly comfort and happiness. On the contrary, our leader voluntarily walked to the cross, giving up His own life to save ours. He entrusted Himself to the Father and willingly received all that came with His submission. He, in fact, embraced the pain because He knew what was coming on the other side.

Our redemption. Our freedom. Our forever with Him in heaven.

Yet, so often we assume God's favor will result in the lessening of (or all-out prevention of) pain. We think being chosen ensures our earthly lives will turn out well. We think being part of the kingdom of God will allow us to sidestep worldly wrongs like injustice, brokenness, sadness, sickness, loneliness ... even though Jesus experienced every one of those things to the greatest possible degree.

Peter called Him the "living stone rejected by men." But he also called Him the "cornerstone chosen and precious" and declared that "whoever believes in him will not be put to shame."

You will not be put to shame.

You will not be put to shame.

You will not be put to shame.

"For this reason the Father loves me, because I lay down my life that I may take it up again. No one takes it from me, but I lay it down of my own accord. I have authority to lay it down, and I have authority to take it up again. This charge I have received from my Father."
John 10:17–18

"For to this you have been called, because Christ also suffered for you, leaving you an example, so that you might follow in his steps. He committed no sin, neither was deceit found in his mouth. When he was reviled, he did not revile in return; when he suffered, he did not threaten, but continued entrusting himself to him who judges justly. He himself bore our sins in his body on the tree, that we might die to sin and live to righteousness. By his wounds you have been healed. For you were straying like sheep, but have now returned to the Shepherd and Overseer of your souls."
1 Peter 2:21–25

"But he was pierced for our transgressions; he was crushed for our iniquities; upon him was the chastisement that brought us peace, and with his wounds we are healed."
Isaiah 53:5

"And he began to teach them that the Son of Man must suffer many things and be rejected by the elders and the chief priests and the scribes and be killed, and after three days rise again."
Mark 8:31

"Then Pilate took Jesus and flogged him. And the soldiers twisted together a crown of thorns and put it on his head and arrayed him in a purple robe. They came up to him, saying, 'Hail, King of the Jews!' and struck him with their hands. Pilate went out again and said to them, 'See, I am bringing him out to you that you may know that I find no guilt in him.' So Jesus came out, wearing the crown of thorns and the purple robe. Pilate said to them, 'Behold the man!' When the chief priests and the officers saw him, they cried out, 'Crucify him, crucify him!'"
John 19:1–6

Roman flogging:
whipping with leather strips that had small pieces of metal or bone at the ends intended for tearing flesh.

Crucify:
capital punishment wherein the victim was nailed to a cross or large wooden beam and hung until eventual death.

"In the days of his flesh, Jesus offered up prayers and supplications, with loud cries and tears, to him who was able to save him from death, and he was heard because of his reverence. Although he was a son, he learned obedience through what he suffered."
Hebrews 5:7–8

Your Turn

1. Spend some time contemplating all the ways Jesus suffered while living on earth, along with the verses in the margin. What strikes you most about the hardship He faced?

Vindicated

If you follow Jesus, you're like a living stone being built into a dwelling place of worship:

"So then you are no longer strangers and aliens, but you are fellow citizens with the saints and members of the household of God, built on the foundation of the apostles and prophets, Christ Jesus himself being the cornerstone, in whom the whole structure, being joined together, grows into a holy temple in the Lord. In him you also are being built together into a dwelling place for God by the Spirit" (Eph. 2:19–22).

If you follow Jesus, you're heaven-bound where pain and suffering will be no more:

"And I heard a loud voice from the throne saying, 'Behold, the dwelling place of God is with man. He will dwell with them, and they will be his people, and God himself will be with them as their God. He will wipe away every tear from their eyes, and death shall be no more, neither shall there be mourning, nor crying, nor pain anymore, for the former things have passed away'" (Rev. 21:3–4).

If you follow Jesus, your faith in Him will soon become sight:

"For we know in part and we prophesy in part, but when the perfect comes, the partial will pass away. When I was a child, I spoke like a child, I thought like a child, I reasoned like a child. When I became a man, I gave up childish ways. For now we see in a mirror dimly, but then face to face. Now I know in part; then I shall know fully, even as I have been fully known" (1 Cor. 13:9–12).

If you obey Jesus, your faithfulness will be rewarded:

"Blessed are you when others revile you and persecute you and utter all kinds of evil against you falsely on my account. Rejoice and be glad, for your reward is great in heaven, for so they persecuted the prophets who were before you" (Matt. 5:11–12).

For Bible Nerds (like us) Who Want to Know

Perhaps it should be no surprise that Peter—whose name means "rock"—has a section in his letter about stones! He referred to Jesus as "a living stone rejected by men but in the sight of God chosen and precious" (1 Pet. 2:4) and to believers who "like living stones are being built up as a spiritual house" (v. 5). Meaning, the personal devotion of individual believers to Jesus results in a community that is being built up together into a place of worship.

Growing Christians grow together.

In 1 Peter 2:4–8, the apostle cited several Old Testament passages that also utilize a building metaphor and the use of stones. In Isaiah 28:16, God announced His forthcoming work of salvation: "Behold, I am the one who has laid as a foundation in Zion, a stone, a tested stone, a precious cornerstone, of a sure foundation: 'Whoever believes will not be in haste.'"

Peter then paraphrased that verse and identified Jesus as God's salvation, and reiterated that those who believe would not be put to shame.

But while Isaiah 28 references the good news about those who believe in Jesus as the cornerstone, Peter went on to cite Psalm 118:22 and the bad news for those who do not believe: "The stone that the builders rejected has become the cornerstone."

If you surrender to Jesus, you will forevermore be part of His kingdom, which will not fail. Or fall. Or end:

"And behold, you will conceive in your womb and bear a son, and you shall call his name Jesus. He will be great and will be called the Son of the Most High. And the Lord God will give to him the throne of his father David, and he will reign over the house of Jacob forever, and of his kingdom there will be no end" (Luke 1:31–33).

And someday soon, this broken world will be fully and completely eclipsed by the new one Jesus promises to bring with Him when He returns:

"Then I saw a new heaven and a new earth, for the first heaven and the first earth had passed away, and the sea was no more. And I saw the holy city, new Jerusalem, coming down out of heaven from God, prepared as a bride adorned for her husband.... And he who was seated on the throne said, 'Behold, I am making all things new.' Also he said, 'Write this down, for these words are trustworthy and true.' And he said to me, 'It is done! I am the Alpha and the Omega, the beginning and the end. To the thirsty I will give from the spring of the water of life without payment. The one who conquers will have this heritage, and I will be his God and he will be my son.' ... Then the angel showed me the river of the water of life, bright as crystal, flowing from the throne of God and of the Lamb through the middle of the street of the city; also, on either side of the river, the tree of life with its twelve kinds of fruit, yielding its fruit each month. The leaves of the tree were for the healing of the nations. No longer will there be anything accursed, but the throne of God and of the Lamb will be in it, and his servants will worship him. They will see his face, and his name will be on their foreheads. And night will be no more. They will need no light of lamp or sun, for the Lord God will be their light, and they will reign forever and ever" (Rev. 21:1–2, 5–7; 22:1–5).

Which means, you will not be put to shame:

"Though now for a little while, if necessary, you have been grieved by various trials, so that the tested genuineness of your faith—more precious than gold that perishes though it is tested by fire—may be found to result in praise and glory and honor at the revelation of Jesus Christ" (1 Pet. 1:6–7).

And now we've come full circle.

Your Turn

2. How does the hope of heaven impact the way you feel about your current circumstances?

3. How does the hope of heaven bestow steadiness, dignity, and purpose upon your life, no matter your circumstances?

4. How should the hope of heaven change your priorities while you endure your circumstances?

All the Things

"And we know that for those who love God

all things work together for good,

for those who are called according to his purpose."

Romans 8:28

Disillusioned:
to be disappointed in
someone or something
that is discovered to be
less "good" than what
we thought it would be.

Our human tendency is to resist suffering. To see it as a bad thing. To blame God for it, or to become disillusioned by the things He allows in our lives. To writhe in frustration. To fixate on what we don't have. To grieve without hope. To pull away from the One who wants to comfort us, help us, heal us, change us.

But when it comes to hardship, perhaps we've been responding all wrong.

Jesus didn't resist the cross. Or, for that matter, any of the trials He endured before it:

"He had no beauty or majesty to attract us to him, nothing in his appearance that we should desire him. He was despised and rejected by mankind, a man of suffering, and familiar with pain. Like one from whom people hide their faces he was despised, and we held him in low esteem. Surely he took up our pain and bore our suffering, yet we considered him punished by God, stricken by him, and afflicted. But he was pierced for our transgressions, he was crushed for our iniquities; the punishment that brought us peace was on him, and by his wounds we are healed" (Isa. 53:2–5 NIV).

Indeed, Christ willingly submitted Himself to God's plan for mankind's salvation, knowing that all of it would be used for our good and His glory—because God is faithful and *can't be anything but* good and loving and purposeful and sovereign and present and perfect in knowledge and wholly committed to our sanctification.

And He loves you.

And He sees you.

And He's for you.

And He's got you in the palm of His hand and at the center of His will.

Oh that we'd believe all of it and rest in God's wisdom, surrender to His will, and receive what He has for us, both now and forevermore.

Your Turn

5. In what ways are you still resisting suffering?

6. Reread Romans 8:28. What good have you seen come from your own suffering, whether now or in the past?

For Bible Nerds (like us) Who Want to Know

Unlike modern English writers, ancient authors like Peter had no qualms about mixing their metaphors. In Peter's letter, he went from eating metaphors (spiritual food and tasting) to a building metaphor (stones for constructing). Meaning, those who follow Jesus are like living stones who are being built into a spiritual house of worship, Christ being the cornerstone of that building. Of course, in ancient construction, the cornerstone was the most necessary and vital point in a structure's foundation for measuring, leveling, erecting, and ensuring the rest of the building.

Thus, Jesus is the cornerstone upon which the entire house of God is being joined together.

He's also the Lamb. In Matthew 25:31-46, Jesus said that those who follow Him are like sheep, and He explained how He'll separate those who truly believed ("the sheep") from those who merely claimed to believe but were not transformed ("the goats").

He's also living water.

"Whoever drinks of the water that I will give him will never be thirsty again. The water that I will give him will become in him a spring of water welling up to eternal life" (John 4:14).

He's also the bread of life.

"I am the bread of life; whoever comes to me shall not hunger, and whoever believes in me shall never thirst" (John 6:35).

He's also the light of the world.

Jesus said, "I am the light of the world. Whoever follows me will not walk in darkness, but will have the light of life" (John 8:12).

7. How might you begin to surrender to and receive *all* that God has for you?

Receive

> "Therefore, since we are surrounded by such a great cloud of
> witnesses, let us throw off everything that hinders and the sin
> that so easily entangles. And let us run with perseverance the
> race marked out for us, fixing our eyes on Jesus, the pioneer and
> perfecter of faith. For the joy set before him he endured the
> cross, scorning its shame, and sat down at the right hand of the
> throne of God. Consider him who endured such opposition
> from sinners, so that you will not grow weary and lose heart."
>
> Hebrews 12:1–3 (NIV)

When suffering is put in the light of everything God has promised, and everything He's faithfully doing, the hard things we experience on earth lose some of their vigor and significance, don't they? That's not to say our pain isn't real. It is. In fact, no one understands that more than Jesus, "the pioneer and perfector of our faith."

But since this world is passing away like a vapor (James 4:14), and because God is good and all His plans are for the good of those who love Him (Ps. 84:11), we can resolve to receive all He has for us while we're here. As we do, we can trust Him to go before, behind, and beside us (Deut. 31:8; Ps. 139:1–3); to provide peace and wisdom beyond our usual capacity or understanding (Phil. 4:6–7; James 1:5); to continue loving us beyond our comprehension and in all the fullness for which we were created (Eph. 3:18–19).

Like our beloved Savior—and for the joy set before us—we can endure. As we do, we can rely on Him to renew our strength so we don't grow weary and we don't lose heart. After all, we've been established by the Cornerstone, and our foundation and future are secure.

He *is* our joy.

Your Turn

8. In what ways is the goodness of the Lord eclipsing your suffering?

Prayer Focus

Praise Jesus for entrusting Himself to the Father, and for willingly receiving God's plan for Him on earth. Thank Him for His promise that you won't be put to shame, and that your faith is well founded. Ask for His peace that surpasses understanding and for greater faith courage to receive all God has for you on earth. And for joy.

Sample Prayer

Oh give thanks to the LORD, for he is good; for his steadfast love endures forever! Let Israel say, "His steadfast love endures forever." Let the house of Aaron say, "His steadfast love endures forever." Let those who fear the LORD say, "His steadfast love endures forever." Out of my distress I called on the LORD; the LORD answered me and set me free. The LORD is on my side; I will not fear. What can man do to me? The LORD is on my side as my helper; I shall look in triumph on those who hate me. It is better to take refuge in the LORD than to trust in man. It is better to take refuge in the LORD than to trust in princes.... I thank you that you have answered me and have become my salvation. The stone that the builders rejected has become the cornerstone. This is the LORD's doing; it is marvelous in our eyes. This is the day that the LORD has made; let us rejoice and be glad in it. Save us, we pray, O LORD! O LORD, we pray, give us success! Blessed is he who comes in the name of the LORD! We bless you from the house of the LORD. The LORD is God, and he has made his light to shine upon us. Bind the festal sacrifice with cords, up to the horns of the altar! You are my God, and I will give thanks to you; you are my God; I will extol you. Oh give thanks to the LORD, for he is good; for his steadfast love endures forever!

Psalm 118:1–9, 21–29

BETHANY—HOUSE OF LAZARUS—MAIN ROOM

(Dinner is served at the house of Lazarus, who reclines at table with Jesus. The disciples, the women, and Zebedee are all there. The only person missing is Mary B.)

PETER: So, Lazarus, six days to go. Have you selected your lamb?

LAZARUS: Yes, he's out back. I just need to perform the rites and bring him in. *(to Jesus)* Whenever You're here, I seem to neglect all my duties.

JESUS: You're not neglectful. We have to soak up our time together.

(There is a KNOCK at the door.)

LAZARUS *(to Martha)*: Are we expecting someone?

MARTHA *(getting up)*: Well, no one knows where Mary is, but she wouldn't knock.

PETER: We should be careful who we let in these days.

LAZARUS: Agreed.

MARTHA *(opening the door)*: Arnán!

ARNÁN: Martha.

MARTHA: Much better circumstances than the last time you came to my door. Come in.

ARNÁN: Thank you.

(As he steps in with Shmuel and Yussif, Lazarus gets up to greet them.)

ARNÁN (CONT'D): Lazarus. Rabbi. Please, I don't mean to interrupt. I've brought with me a member of the Sanhedrin.

JESUS: Shmuel.

SHMUEL *(surprised and also relieved)*: You ... remember me?

JESUS: Of course I do.

(The disciples look spooked. They've got history.)

ARNÁN: Well, I am relieved I have not made a great mistake in bringing him here. And a newcomer to the Sanhedrin, this is—

TAMAR: Yussif.

(Everyone turns to her in surprise.)

ANDREW *(to Jesus)*: He gave us warning in Jotapata that people were looking for You.

(News to Shmuel.)

SHMUEL: I was looking for You.

JESUS *(smiling)*: Well, you've found Me. And congratulations to you both for your appointments ... Capernaum's finest! Please, will you join us?

(Disciples scramble to create two more spots at the table.)

JUDAS *(leaning into Peter)*: This is a tremendous opportunity for a strategic alliance.

PETER *(skeptical)*: We'll see.

ARNÁN *(settling in)*: Rabbi, we have reason to believe there is danger lying in wait for You at the highest levels of Temple leadership.

JESUS: I would not have expected that.

(The three visitors look like deer in headlights.)

JESUS (CONT'D): I am joking. Go on.

SHMUEL: Jesus of Nazareth, Your situation has become a matter of life and death.

JESUS: It has always been.

LAZARUS: They tried to stone Him in the Temple courts!

YUSSIF: What we mean is, Your fame has gone beyond fame. Not just many in numbers, but much in debate. Lately it's because of him *(indicating Lazarus)*.

LAZARUS: Oh, I'm sorry, I'll try not to die next time.

JESUS: No, it's all part of the plan.

SHMUEL: Your ruin? That's part of Your plan? Because that's where this is headed.

JESUS: Is that what you've come to tell Me?

SHMUEL *(composing himself)*: You've called Yourself the Son of Man.

PETER: Here we go again ...

SHMUEL: I'm not here to contest that or take offense this time. I'm open.

JESUS: I can tell. I see it in your eyes.

SHMUEL: If You are who You say You are, what is Your plan? The entire city of Jerusalem is eagerly awaiting Your arrival for Passover, some with open arms, others with daggers. Do You have an army we don't know about? If You are ... more than a rabbi ... You will have more than just Rome to overthrow, but also many religious leaders. They will not join You in Your quest.

JUDAS: Perhaps you can help them do so. This is the week.

JESUS: Rabbi Shmuel, what would you like to see? Regardless of *who* ... what is your hope for a Messiah?

SHMUEL: To usher in a new Davidic kingdom that drives out our oppressors and restores justice and glory for Israel.

JESUS: Hmm. Glory.

SHMUEL: Yes. On a glorious throne. With prosperity for all, a new Golden Age, with Israel as a light to the nations, revealing God to the peoples of the world.

JESUS: And you ... what will you do in that day?

SHMUEL *(thrown)*: Worship? Serve, I hope? How could I possibly know until that day comes?

JESUS: I will tell you. When the Son of Man comes in His glory, and all the angels with Him, *then* He will sit on His glorious throne.

(Shmuel nods. This tracks.)

JESUS (CONT'D): Before Him will be gathered all the nations, and He will separate people one from another as a shepherd separates the sheep from the goats. And He will place the sheep on His right, but the goats on the left. Then the King will say to those on His right, "Come, you who are blessed by My Father, inherit the kingdom that has been prepared for you from the foundation of the world. For I was hungry and you gave Me food, I was thirsty and you gave Me drink, I was a stranger and you welcomed Me, I was naked and you clothed Me, I was sick and you visited Me, I was in prison and you came to Me." Then the righteous will answer Him, saying, "Lord, when did we do these things for You?" Then the King will answer, "Truly, I say to you, as you did it to one of the least of these My brothers, you did it to Me."

(Surprised looks all around. Shmuel shifts uncomfortably.)

JESUS (CONT'D): Then He will say to those on His left, "Depart from Me, for I was hungry and you gave Me no food, I was thirsty and you gave Me no drink, I was a stranger and you did not welcome Me, naked and you did not clothe Me, sick and in prison and you did not visit Me." Then they also will answer, saying, "Lord, when did we see You hungry or thirsty or a stranger or naked or sick or in prison, and did not minister to You?"

(Judas looks troubled.)

JESUS (CONT'D): Then He will answer them, saying, "As you did not do it to one of the least of these, you did not do it to Me."

(The entire room is in various states of wonder. Finally, Shmuel manages—)

SHMUEL: This is a hard teaching.

JESUS: I do not know how to make it less so.

SHMUEL: The Son of Man, the Messiah, is identified with the lowest of all people? The hungry, the poor, the stranger?

JESUS: It's been what I've been preaching from My opening sentence on the mount.

SHMUEL: But what of all the Torah requirements and traditions upheld by our forefathers?

JESUS: The prophet Micah distilled such things down to their essence, and you overlooked it: "He has told you, O man, what is good; and what does the Lord require of you but to do justice … and to love kindness … and to walk humbly with your God?"

SHMUEL: Yes, but how do you harmonize that with the parting conclusion of Qohelet in the Ketuvim? "The end of the matter; all has been heard. Fear God and keep His commandments, for this is the whole duty of man."

Qohelet = speaker.

Ketuvim = the body of literature Ecclesiastes is included in.

JESUS: A new commandment I give you, that you love one another, just as I have loved you.

(He distributes His gaze among the disciples.)

JESUS (CONT'D): By this all people will know that you are My disciples, that you have love for one another.

SHMUEL: What of the Temple, the sacrifices, the law, the feasts? Are not keeping these how the nations will know we are God's people?

JESUS: The Temple, the sacrifices, the law, the feasts ... all fulfilled in Me.

SHMUEL: You would do away with them?

JESUS: I said fulfilled, not done away.

SHMUEL: I don't understand the difference.

JESUS: Keeping the law is a response to God's love. But now that I am here—

(They are interrupted by the arrival of Mary of Bethany, teary-eyed and trembling, holding the alabaster jar. No one is sure what to do. Martha approaches.)

MARTHA *(quietly)*: What is the matter? Where have you been?

SHMUEL *(turning back to Jesus)*: You were saying about the law?

(Everyone else is wide eyed as Mary B proceeds toward Jesus. She kneels at His feet.)

SHMUEL (CONT'D): What's going on? Who is this?

LAZARUS: My sister, Mary.

(The jar Mary is holding has a long, thin neck. After a moment, she breaks it on the floor, prompting gasps from the entire room.)

MARTHA: Mary!

JUDAS *(smelling)*: That's spikenard!

LAZARUS: Mary, what are you doing?

(Their shock only compounds when she, ignoring everyone, starts to anoint Jesus's feet, emptying the full contents. The house is filled with the fragrance, and some can hardly breathe, tears forming from the strength of the aroma.)

SHMUEL *(to Lazarus)*: You're letting your sister touch His feet? That's degrading!

LAZARUS: Have you heard nothing of what the Teacher said?

(The scandal intensifies all around when Mary B removes her head covering.)

SHMUEL: All right, this is enough. Jesus ...

(She begins to dry His feet with her own hair.)

JESUS: Once again, Shmuel, there is no law in Torah commanding a woman to cover her hair. That's just tradition.

SHMUEL: Are You commending her? Excusing her?

YUSSIF: Shmuel, we don't know this family, it's not our place.

MARY B *(through tears)*: Blessed are You, King of the Universe ... for You have done all things well ...

SHMUEL: Yussif, Arnán, we need to leave!

ARNÁN: Now? Rabbi Shmuel, I understand, but we need to—

SHMUEL: She's performing an inappropriate act openly, without shame, and He's allowing it while being called God. We can't be found out to have witnessed it and done nothing!

YUSSIF: An open investigation, you said. Let's see what He says.

JUDAS *(picking up the broken alabaster jar, stunned, unraveling)*: Pure nard ... of the highest quality ... this ... we could have sold this for more than two hundred denarii ...

JESUS: What troubles you, Judas?

JUDAS: Why was this ointment not sold for hundreds of denarii?

SHMUEL: You just told a story about how caring for the poor is akin to caring for the Messiah.

JUDAS: Yes, this could have been given to the poor! This could've been used for anything—supplies, shelter, but this ... this is a waste! *(to Mary B)* Where did you get this money, Mary?

JESUS: Leave her alone! She has done a beautiful thing to Me. For you will always have the poor with you, and whenever you want, you can do good for them. But you will not always have Me.

> "For it stands in Scripture: 'Behold, I am laying in Zion a stone, a cornerstone chosen and precious, and whoever believes in him will not be put to shame.' So the honor is for you who believe ..."
> 1 Peter 2:6–7

(Shmuel looks disgusted. Mary Mother looks heartbroken.)

JESUS (CONT'D): She has done what she could; she has anointed My body beforehand for burial.

NATHANAEL: Burial??

JUDAS: What does that mean?

PETER: Shh—let Him finish!

JESUS: And believe Me, wherever the gospel is proclaimed in the whole world, what she has done will be told in memory of her.

SHMUEL: What Your follower said is right. This act was wasteful, immodest, and completely contradicts everything You said before about the poor and lowly.

LAZARUS: He said they will always have them with us.

SHMUEL: The very notion that such a disgrace would be "proclaimed throughout the world" as part of Your gospel when instead it should be reproached, rebuked, and condemned—it's ... I can't be in the same room as this abomination.

ANDREW: Sounds like a personal problem.

SHMUEL *(turning back at the door and pointing at Jesus)*: I wanted to believe! I came here to give You a chance, and You've ruined it.

JESUS *(compassionately)*: I'm sorry I couldn't help you.

SHMUEL: I'm sorry I couldn't help You.

(He slams the door behind him.)

JUDAS: Rabbi, that is not a man we want to upset if we are looking to unite our people.

(Jesus ignores Judas and looks to Yussif for his reaction. But Yussif only repeats—)

YUSSIF: "For burial"?

(Jesus silently nods.)

"But for those who do not believe, 'The stone that the builders rejected has become the cornerstone,' and 'A stone of stumbling, and a rock of offense.' They stumble because they disobey the word, as they were destined to do."

1 Peter 2:7–8

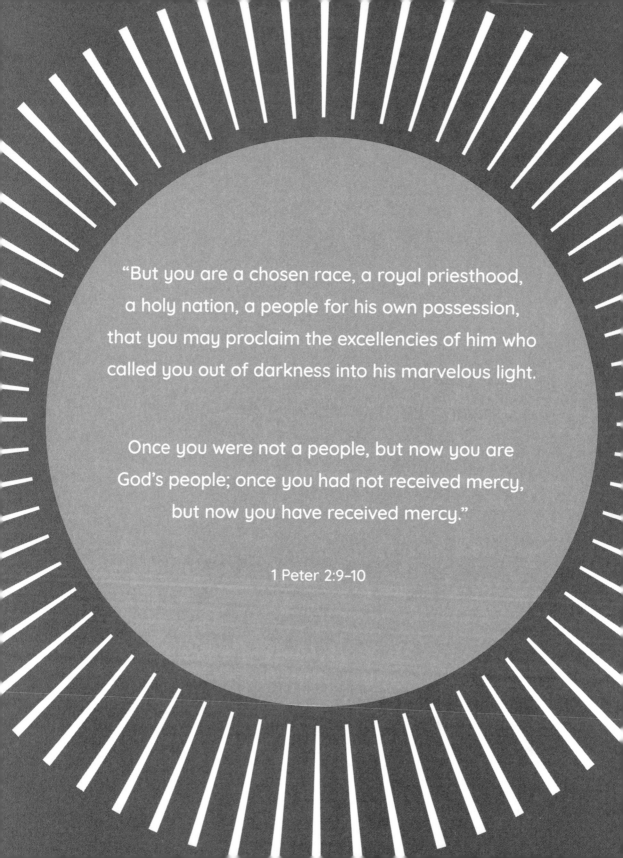

"But you are a chosen race, a royal priesthood, a holy nation, a people for his own possession, that you may proclaim the excellencies of him who called you out of darkness into his marvelous light.

Once you were not a people, but now you are God's people; once you had not received mercy, but now you have received mercy."

1 Peter 2:9–10

CONCLUSION

Peter concluded the first section of his letter to "the elect exiles of the Dispersion" (1 Pet. 1:1) with a statement about their very identity.

And ours.

We are chosen.

We are set apart.

We are cherished.

We are recipients of God's mercy.

We are heralds of His goodness.

We are citizens of heaven.

Like Peter, we can rejoice in trials, in hardship, and yes, *even in suffering* because we understand their purpose in our lives, which is why we fix our eyes on the blessings therein and hold fast to how radically good God is, while we wait on the bigger thing He's doing.

Indeed, the hard things we experience in this short life are *always* eclipsed by the bigger thing God is doing in and through them. So, instead of lamenting our lack, we welcome it.

"Beloved, do not be surprised at the fiery trial when it comes upon you to test you, as though something strange were happening to you. But rejoice insofar as you share Christ's sufferings, that you may also rejoice and be glad when his glory is revealed" (1 Pet. 4:12–13).

Oh that we would trust God with greater anticipation—and even joy—that His perfect, loving, and unfailing plan for our lives is good. Oh that we would embrace our identity in Christ and stand firm in the victory He's already secured. And oh that we, like all the faithful followers of Jesus who came before us, would proclaim the good news of His merciful salvation all the way to heaven.

It is, after all, only a matter of time.

NOTES

NOTES

NOTES

NOTES

NOTES

ABOUT THE AUTHORS

Amanda Jenkins is an author and mother of four. She is the lead creator for *The Chosen*'s extra content, including *The Chosen* devotionals and *The Chosen* children's books *Jesus Loves the Little Children* and *The Shepherd*. She lives in Texas with her kids and husband, Dallas, creator of *The Chosen*.

Dallas Jenkins is a filmmaker, author, and speaker. Over the past twenty years, he has directed and produced over a dozen films for companies such as Warner Brothers, Lionsgate, Universal Studios, and Hallmark Channel. He is now the creator of *The Chosen*, the first-ever multi-season show about the life of Christ and the highest crowd-funded media project of all-time. He lives with his family in Texas where they now film the show.

The official evangelical biblical consultant for *The Chosen* TV series, **Douglas S. Huffman** (PhD, Trinity Evangelical Divinity School) is Professor of New Testament and Associate Dean of Biblical and Theological Studies at Talbot School of Theology (Biola University) in California. Specializing in New Testament Greek, Luke–Acts, and Christian Thought, he is the author of *Verbal Aspect Theory and the Prohibitions in the Greek New Testament* and *The Handy Guide to New Testament Greek*; contributing editor of such books as *God Under Fire: Modern Scholarship Reinvents God*, *How Then Should We Choose? Three Views on God's Will and Decision Making*, and *Christian Contours: How a Biblical Worldview Shapes the Mind and Heart*; and contributor to several theological journals and reference works. Dr. Huffman can be seen on *The Chosen*'s "Bible Roundtables" on *The Chosen* app. He enjoys working with Biola undergraduate students, pointing them to Scripture as God's Word for us today.